THE POWER OF ASSET MAPPING

*How Your Congregation
Can Act on Its Gifts*

LUTHER K. SNOW

The Alban Institute
Herndon, Virginia
www.alban.org

Library of Congress Cataloging-in-Publication Data

Snow, Luther K.
    The power of asset mapping : how your congregation can act on its gifts / Luther K. Snow.
        p. cm.
    ISBN 1-56699-294-X
    1. Church management. 2. Social surveys. 3. Mission of the church. I. Title.

BV652.4.S66 2004
254—dc22

                                                            2004000548

15   14   13   VG   6   7   8   9   10

Contents

Part Three
The WHY: Why Does Asset Mapping Work?

Foreword

THIS BOOK ATTEMPTS to make us believe, once again, in miracles. No, we are not invited to commune with angels or to make a pilgrimage to a weeping virgin. Instead, Luther Snow asks simply that we refocus on our half-full rather than half empty realities, that we appreciate anew our own gifts and capacities and those of our neighbors, that we connect those gifts to one another in creative combinations, and that we activate those connections to strengthen our congregations and communities.

In fact, Luther Snow believes deeply in miracles, because he has witnessed them himself and has helped make them happen. He has seen congregations come to life, members' faith and commitments expand, new ministries being invented. He has discovered for himself—and now leads us to discover—the simple yet miraculous power with which we are already gifted, the power we can experience when we act intentionally with one another.

The "asset mapping" process Snow describes resonates with us both historically and theologically. The living church has always emphasized the importance of faithful stewardship, the full utilization of the gifts and talents of the people of God. The psalmists sing of the abundance made available by a loving and protective God. The prophets continually call not only for the renunciation of sin and idolatry, but for the recognition and celebration of faith-filled worship and actions. And Jesus discovers gifts and capacities in the least likely people—beggars, prostitutes, tax collectors, little children.

With its biblical and historical roots, congregational asset mapping is also related to contemporary developments in the secular community-building movement. In his role as an adjunct faculty member of the Asset-Based Community Development (ABCD) Institute at Northwestern University, Snow has worked with both rural and urban communities to help them discover and mobilize their strengths and resources.

The asset-based approach to development grew out of the recognition that communities, like congregations, can experience cycles of negativity. In fact, many of our culture's most powerful institutions insist that struggling inner-city neighborhoods and rural areas understand themselves as primarily challenged and problematic—ubiquitous "needs surveys" trumpet the "half-empty" realities involving crime rates, dropouts, gangs, drugs, joblessness, and homelessness. While these challenges are all too real, effective community builders have discovered that they do not constitute the ingredients from which solutions are fashioned. Rather, healthy and vital communities are built through a process similar to Snow's congregational asset mapping. It begins with the rediscovery and mapping of a community's resources—the skills and capacities of its residents; the power of local associations and networks; the resources of local public, private and nonprofit institutions; and the physical and economic assets. Sustainable development involves processes that constantly create connections among all of these resources and that harness their collective power behind a compelling vision for the future. Funding and other resources from outside the community do not lead this process; rather, they strengthen an internally driven dynamic.

Snow reports that congregational asset mapping frequently leads to an increase in community-oriented ministries and to building effective relationships both with other congregations and with secular groups. This process of building community connections can also be understood as part of a larger movement. Think, for example, about the range of institutions that in recent years have begun to rediscover the power of these local partnerships—community policing, community schools, and the like.

Finally, Snow suggests that producing miracles in congregations and communities is something every member, and every resident, can do. Congregational asset mapping is not the work of experts or professionals. All of us "ordinary" people can not only participate in it, we can actually lead it. Luther Snow's enthusiasm for the simple three-step process is contagious. He has seen with his own eyes the miraculous results that come from finding peoples' gifts, connecting them to one another, and taking action together. He understands this rich and creative process as one that has in fact produced miracles throughout history but one that perhaps every generation must rediscover for itself. Let this book serve as a powerful invitation for all of us to join the ongoing process of producing miracles together.

John McKnight
Jody Kretzmann

Preface

THIS BOOK IS arranged backwards.

Usually, when we try to explain things, we go from *why* to *how* to *what*. A traditional textbook, self-help manual, or other exposition will generally start by making a case for *why* something deserves our attention. In light of this larger analysis, the author will then propose *how* things should work. At the end, the author will finally discuss *what* specific things we can actually do to implement these ideas.

This book starts with *what*, then reaches *how*, and finally opens up into *why*. I start this book by describing *what* actually happens in congregational asset mapping, including enough information so that you can try it on your own, individually or in groups. I then draw on that experience to discuss *how* asset mapping works in congregations and other groups. From there I open up lessons about *why* asset mapping strengthens faith and community.

I've chosen to arrange the book this way because this is how the structure actually works in congregations and communities of faith. As a consultant, developer, and facilitator who has worked in and among communities of people all my life, I've seen every kind of group process, leadership style, and facilitation method. Asset mapping with congregations has shown me that backwards is better.

If you think about it, the traditional structure is a way of narrowing things down. It's a way of trying to control the complexities of life by screening out many possibilities to arrive at a small number of actions.

Asset mapping is just the opposite. It is a way of opening up possibilities. First we take action, which gives us experience and confidence. Then we reflect on our action, which helps us recognize new actions we can take to build on what we've done. Every action opens up new possibilities, which leads to more learning and more action.

Now that I have witnessed the success of this backwards approach, I no longer start a workshop or a consulting session with a speech about assets. Instead, I begin with the Quick and Simple Congregational Asset-Mapping

Experience (chapter 2). As we experience asset mapping, we learn for ourselves how God opens up our faith and empowers us to act in community.

By doing things backwards, I'm trying to turn over control and open myself up to the unexpected and amazing gifts of God. I hope this book will work backwards for you, too.

COPYRIGHT AND REPRODUCTION NOTICE

The resources in *The Power of Asset Mapping* are intended for use in the congregation in a variety of settings. Because many of these resources are used most effectively within the context in which they are presented in this book, I recommend that congregations purchase copies of the book for each individual in small-group contexts. Due to copyright protection issues, these materials may not be reproduced in any form without written permission from the Alban Institute.

Recognizing that many congregations will want to reproduce some of these materials for use in larger-group settings, the Alban Institute has made several of these resources available for free download from the Alban Web site. These resources have been formatted for easy and clear printing on 8-1/2" x 11" paper and may be printed and reproduced in limited quantities for private use in the congregation without obtaining written permission. For more information, go to http://www.alban.org/BookDetails.asp?ID=1811.

Acknowledgments

WHAT I HAVE LEARNED about faith and community comes from working with people like you. I have worked with hundreds of congregations and communities and thousands of community leaders from across the United States and in Canada. The stories, people, and situations you read about in this book are drawn from my recollections of spirited meetings and discussions I have attended over the years on critical community issues. For sharing the lessons of faith and community with me, I give thanks to all the good people trying to make things happen in church basements and community meeting halls across the land.

I thank Jody Kretzmann and John McKnight of the Asset-Based Community Development (ABCD) Institute at Northwestern University for encouraging me to write and for showing me the spirit of open-ended sharing. I also recognize my colleagues in the adjunct faculty network of asset builders, including especially faith builders like the Rev. James Conn, who is contributing to the United Methodist efforts in southern California; the Rev. Damon Lynch of New Prospect Missionary Baptist Church in Cincinnati, Ohio; the Rev. Craig J. Lewis, catalyst of several Evangelical Lutheran Church of America efforts in Minnesota; Mr. Richard Townsell, executive director of the Lawndale Christian Development Corporation; and Dr. Mary Nelson of Bethel New Life in Chicago. I also know and appreciate Richard and Mary for their leadership in the international Christian Community Development Association.

For the inspiration and collaboration that sparked and formed congregational asset mapping, I thank the participants in the National Demonstration Project on Congregational Asset Mapping, sponsored by the churchwide offices of the Evangelical Lutheran Church in America. I am indebted to Chris Grumm, now executive director of the National Women's Funding Network, for engaging me in that effort. Deborah Puntenney of the ABCD Institute was a key collaborator on the development of The Quick and Simple Experience. Rick Deines helped pulled together the three participating congregations in the Greater Milwaukee Synod. And I especially wish to thank the clergy and lay leaders from the seven congregations who participated in the project:

> Living Waters, Lino Lakes. Minnesota, led by Pastor Tim Nelson
> Prince of Peace, Seatac, Washington, led by Pastor Steve Grumm
> Divine Word, Milwaukee, Wisconsin, led by Pastor Kris Erdmann
> Florist Avenue, Milwaukee, Wisconsin, led by Pastor Cheri Johnson
> Pentecost, Milwaukee, Wisconsin, led by Pastor Steve Wohlfiel
> First Lutheran, Farmersburg, Iowa, and
> McGregor Lutheran, McGregor, Iowa, both led by Pastor Bruce Hanson

I am grateful to Myrna Sheie, executive assistant to the bishop, who staffed the National Demonstration Project and who has supported and encouraged my efforts ever since, including the publication of this book.

Among the community groups and leaders who formed my sense of community dynamics, I thank the people of the Hyde Park-Kenwood Community Conference, where I got a start as a tenant organizer, and the members and board leaders of the Community Workshop on Economic Development and the Chicago Association of Neighborhood Development Corporations, who taught me about the dynamics of coalitions. I give thanks to the rural community leaders from Arkansas to South Carolina, from Kentucky to California, who shared with me the asset-based faith of the countryside that I reported on in *The Organization of Hope: A Workbook for Rural Asset-Based Community Development* (Evanston, Ill.: ABCD Institute, 2001; distributed by ACTA Publishers).

And I thank Mary Nelson, whom I named above, Kate Lane, and all the good people of the dynamic and faith-based community development corporation called Bethel New Life, who showed me so much of what you find on these pages about faith and community.

I thank my editor, Beth Gaede, for challenging me to go farther than I thought possible, and for her good cheer and bright ideas.

And most of all, I thank my wife, Lise Kildegaard, editor, colleague, and best friend, who shows me signs of God's grace every day.

PART ONE

The WHAT

What Is Congregational Asset Mapping?

CONGREGATIONAL ASSET MAPPING starts by looking at assets. When we think about it, we recognize that we have been given gifts in abundance. Our cup is not half-empty; it is half-full. That is something to be thankful for. That half-full cup gives us power to do good things for ourselves, our neighbors, and in the world.

When we look at the half-full cup, we recognize and redis-cover our assets and the abundance of God's gifts. We find an exciting, new, and positive energy to break us out of the nega-tive cycles of need, dependency, and inaction that people in congregations sometimes experience.

And that's just the start! We soon discover that our own gifts and assets are made valuable by connecting them to the gifts of others. Beyond need and charity, we find affinity and partnership. Our stewardship is active, and our actions together grow and open toward the will of God. In short, when we map our assets we find the grace between our gifts. Try it yourself and see.

Chapter 1

A Personal Asset Starter

Asset mapping happens between people. It is a group activity or, better yet, like a snowball rolled through the snow by a group of children, asset mapping spreads and grows among widening groups of people. In this book you will find practical methods and lessons for "starting a snowball" in your congregation.

At the heart of asset mapping is a personal transformation: learning or relearning to see the cup as half-full. That's something you can start to experience right now, with a pencil and the pages of this book.

Begin with Basic Assets

What is your cup half-full of? What do you have to be thankful for? To begin with, you have basic assets. The physical objects you hold dear. Your own talents and skills. Your family or friends or the groups you belong to. Your eco-

What is your cup half-full of?
What do you have to be thankful for?

nomic assets—what you spend or save or sell. Let's start with those. Fill out this Personal Asset Starter and see what comes to mind.

This is just a first glance at the assets you are most aware of. Write down whatever comes to your mind:

Physical Assets

■ What are some physical things that you value?

_____

_____

_____

Individual Assets

■ What are you good at?
■ What do you know something about?

_____

_____

_____

Associational Assets

■ Who are the people you know or care about?
■ What groups of people do you belong to?

_____

_____

_____

Institutional Assets

■ Where do you work or volunteer?
■ What institutions make decisions that affect you?

_____

_____

_____

Economic Assets

■ What do you do to make money?
■ What do you spend money on?

_____

_____

_____

Congratulations. You just recognized and affirmed some of your assets. When you recognize even a few of your gifts, strengths, or assets, you are looking at the half-full cup. That's a great start.

---

*Recognizing even a few
of your assets is a start.*

For many people, taking even a small step like this starts to feel fresh and uplifting. So often, we make lists of things we haven't done, problems we haven't fixed, and complaints we haven't addressed. We get so accustomed to dealing with negatives that we forget what it feels like to focus on positives. Just looking at assets, then, you might feel set free.

But you've only scratched the surface. You have many more assets than this.

These categories of Basic Assets are drawn from the work of asset-building pioneers John McKnight and Jody Kretzmann. They define the following five assets types:

1. Physical assets: things that you can touch and see, from land and equipment to natural beauty and the environment.
2. Individual assets: the talents, skills, and experiences of individuals.
3. Associational assets: voluntary groups and networks of people, from the more formally structured volunteer associations (like a service club) to informally gathered groups (like the people who meet for coffee on Tuesday mornings).
4. Institutions: agencies, corporations, and other organizations with budgets and staff. These might be nonprofit (like a hospital) or for-profit (like a manufacturing firm) or public (like a government agency).
5. Economic assets: community assets involving money, such as our spending power, our investments, and our capacities to produce goods and services for money.

LOOK FOR HIDDEN ASSETS

The value of asset mapping starts to grow when we look harder, dig deeper, or broaden our view. Like when we peel back the layers of an onion, we find assets that we did not think of at first. Those are the assets that often present us with new opportunities.

Every person is different. Individuals can use various techniques to see past their own blind spots and discover assets that were hidden from view. Let's try a few approaches and asset starter questions and see what you discover beneath the surface.

Open Up

I once listened to a speech by Mark Hanson, presiding bishop of the Evangelical Lutheran Church in America, in which he talked about how they used to run church council meetings where he was a parish pastor. Instead of the usual business agenda, they would get most things done by prayer, Bible study, and discussions of faith. And they would open every meeting with a question: "What signs of God's grace have you witnessed lately?" This is perhaps the most valuable asset starter question of all and one that is sure to open up our thinking.

■ **What signs of God's grace have you witnessed lately?**

_____

_____

_____

Dig Deeper

Some gifts are so central, immediate, or widespread that we take them for granted. And yet these are sometimes the most valuable assets.

Halfway through an asset discovery process in a gorgeous rural community, one person thought to identify the scenic view of town. The light bulbs went on for other participants, who lifted up the natural resources in their area. In an inner-city church, someone recognized the value of the church's location. That got other people thinking about the value of the church building being visible to traffic and accessible to public transportation. It might surprise you to know how many churchgoing participants forget about all the

Bibles their congregations has! But once people recognize that asset, ideas emerge for creative ways to share the Word.

Are there things that are so close to you that they are harder to see at first?

Other gifts are out of sight, out of mind. These are gifts we overlook because they are out of the ordinary or we just don't come across them very often. As a result, these are often the most interesting assets, the ones that create a spark when people are thinking of ways to use their gifts.

I worked with a rural congregation that initially overlooked their other church building! This second church building was located in the countryside near a beautiful old cemetery, a remainder of a previous merger between two congregations. Recognizing this overlooked asset got that congregation thinking about ways to build on their history and culture by having special services

---

*Intriguing possibilities come alive
when we connect our gifts across
the circles of our lives.*

---

in the old sanctuary. They started thinking they could reclaim and use assets that they had overlooked before.

■ **What are some gifts you take for granted?**

■ **If you asked someone what some of your gifts are, what would the person say?**

■ **What are some strengths and assets that you don't often see or use?**

_____

_____

_____

Think Bigger

Some gifts we miss because we think they "don't go here." We associate certain things with our personal lives, for example, and certain other things with our work or public lives. We might put church in a whole category of its own, with its own day of the week, circle of people, and activities.

But intriguing possibilities come alive when we connect our gifts across the circles of our lives. Several people in one congregation liked fishing. They used that asset to create a series of Bible studies, social events, and worship services around stories of fish in the Bible! The energy this gave the congregation surprised everyone. Opportunities can emerge from assets drawn from unexpected places.

■ What are some gifts that you might have thought don't go here?

■ What are some gifts you have that people in your family, circle of friends, congregation, or community don't get to see very often?

_____

_____

_____

FIND THE ASSETS INSIDE NEEDS

Now you might be asking, But what about needs? Thinking of gifts and assets is all very fine, but there are real hurts out here. We feel strong needs in our own lives, and more than that, we know some people have needs more desperate and severe than our own.

This is an important subject that we are going to cover in some detail throughout this book. For now, you should know that asset mapping does not stand somehow in contrast to compassion or care. On the contrary, asset mapping is a way to put compassion and care into action. Every need points to something we care about. That thing that we care about is always an asset. Here are some ways to think about those assets inside the needs.

See What You See in a Crisis

Assets are easiest to see in a crisis. If a family is burned out of their home by a fire, for example, don't people pull together around them? The crisis makes the community remember that every family is important. That's an asset. People rush to protect that family. They provide clothing, food, money, work, a place to stay—whatever assets they can think of. And in the process, the community rediscovers some of those assets they take for granted. They see the gifts of community they share with each other in faith.

■ Think about a crisis you have seen or experienced. What assets did the crisis bring out?

_____

_____

_____

Look inside Needs

Inside every need is an asset. Members of one congregation thought they were in need of private tutoring for kids until they realized that they were gifted with both children and people who care about children. They were able to start their own after-school program in their church, which strengthened the congregation in many ways.

When you think of a need, deficiency, or obstacle, don't simply disregard it because it is negative. Transform your thinking about needs. Flip it around. Find the valuable asset it represents. Consider, what is the thing that you care so much about?

■ What gifts do you sometimes see as needs?

■ When you focus on a specific need, what is the asset you are caring about?

_____

_____

_____

Sense Power from Abundance

What have we started here? So far all we have done is identify and list gifts and assets. The real power of asset mapping is in taking practical, immediate action.

If you are like me, you are starting to feel this potential already. Look at all the assets you've listed. Do the number and variety surprise you? And this list isn't even the end. It's only the beginning.

More and different gifts come to us as we consider them over time. Indeed, we may take our whole lives learning to count our blessings. Surely, there's not room here to list even a large portion of our gifts. And that's all right—asset mapping isn't meant to produce a whole list, or even a representative one. It's really about practicing a way of thinking, looking at our half-full cup, appreciating God's abundance—and using it.

Already you can get the sense of this mindset, the strength that comes from asset thinking:

- You are not caught in a negative trap. You can *choose* to see the positive.

- You have been given an *abundance* of gifts to use. Recognizing all these gifts, you feel empowered to act.

Now let's look at where asset recognition takes us. Asset mapping isn't something we do for its own sake. Identifying assets gives us the opportunity to *act*. We act by connecting our assets with other assets—that means connecting with other people.

WIDEN YOUR CIRCLE

As you've been identifying gifts and assets, you might have been asking yourself, "Which assets am I considering? My personal assets? My family's assets? My congregation's? My community's?" Yes, this is a Personal Asset Starter. But you belong to many groups of people. In a sense, your family's assets are your assets, as are the assets of the congregation or the community you belong to.

When you ask which assets to consider, you have had an insight into the power of asset mapping. Asset mapping widens our circle of identity and interest, from *mine* to *ours* to *all of ours*.

Try thinking again about your assets, this time stretching your focus. Reconsider the topics addressed in any of the asset starter questions—surface assets, signs of God's grace, gifts we see as needs, and so forth. Only now, think about these assets in widening circles. Consider yourself and the groups you connect with.

■ What are some personal assets that are yours alone?

_____

_____

_____

■ What are some of your family's assets?

_____

_____

_____

■ What are some of your congregation's assets?

_____

_____

_____

■ What are some of your community's assets?

_____

_____

_____

CONNECT THE DOTS

As you identify your assets and widen your circle of vision, two simple but powerful points become clearer:

- You have gifts and interests.

- Other people also have gifts and interests.

We soon discover that our own gifts and assets are made valuable by connecting them to the gifts of others. Asset-building pioneer John McKnight once said to me, "Development is about creating a new link between two or more existing assets." Asset mapping isn't just looking at our gifts and feeling good about them. God didn't give us talents to bury in the backyard.

We are all stewards of God's gifts. Asset mapping provides us with a clearer understanding of our gifts. We can then connect our gifts with those of others and make something new. Connecting the Dots is a simple yet profound expression of active stewardship.

Connecting the Dots is like the old-fashioned barn raising. When early settlers set up a farm or ranch, they did not have the luxury of focusing on their needs. They had to use the gifts they had to get things done. One neighbor had some timber and another neighbor had some carpentry equipment. Several people had individual skills in carpentry. Some could lift and carry. Some could cook. The farmer had an economic asset—the farm. The people put these things together and had a barn raising. They connected several assets to get things done, and created a new asset in the process.

These days, we might do something very similar to build a Habitat for Humanity house or even build a church addition. In a larger sense, connecting the dots like this represents the way we get things done together in faith and life.

Connecting the dots is an excellent group experience, and we'll get to that very soon. But there is one way you can try this for this personal asset starting experience. Let's try that now.

Think back.

Think about some of the successes you've experienced. Consider the good things that have come about in your personal life, family, congregation, or community.

Deconstruct one or more of those successes. Think of the pieces that were put together to make things happen.

■ **What assets got connected to make that success?**

We all have gifts and interests. When you and I connect our gifts and interests with each other, we create something new. Your gain is my gain is our gain. When we map our assets, we find the grace *between* our gifts.

The strength behind congregational asset mapping isn't new to any of us. Asset mapping models a way of thinking and acting that we know and feel almost instinctively. It's how we exercise our faithfulness with other people. Asset mapping lifts up the power of our faithfulness in community and helps us exercise it.

Chapter 2

The Quick and Simple Congregational Asset-Mapping Experience

THE PERSONAL ASSET STARTER gives you a taste of asset mapping at an individual level. The power of asset mapping builds as we relate to each other in small groups and in a larger community. What does doing asset mapping with other people look and feel like?

With the help of other asset-building leaders, I have developed a sample asset-building process that enables groups of people to experience asset mapping together. The process evolved out of many consultations with congregations and other groups. It is fast and easy. It is also the single most inspiring group process I have ever witnessed.

The Quick and Simple Congregational Asset-Mapping Experience is something you can try with a group of people in about an hour. You can facilitate this process yourself, using the following instructions as a guide.

Right now, don't worry about the details. You will find plenty of how and why advice and answers in parts 2 and 3. You will also learn from experience as you try out this process.

Read through the next few pages to get a picture of *what* asset mapping is like with other people.

Even better, use this guide right away to try out the Quick and Simple Experience with a group in your congregation or community. It is actually easier and more powerful to experience asset mapping than to talk about it! Then come back to the rest of this book with your own ideas and questions. Learning by doing is part of what asset mapping is all about.

An Overview

How Long Will This Take?
As little as an hour. If you have more time, you can use that too.

Who Can Do This?
Any group in your congregation, from 6 people to 600 (or more).

What groups will you try asset mapping with?
- The whole congregation
- Church board
- Planning committee
- Youth group
- Women's group
- Men's group
- Bible study group
- Ecumenical project
- Stewardship team
- Bowling team

It could be you will start with one and end up involving many groups as asset mapping catches on.

What Will We Do Exactly?
Basically you'll do three things:
1. *Recognize Your Assets.* Look at your half-full cup to identify many of your congregation's assets and strengths.
2. *Connect the Dots.* Link some of these assets together to brainstorm *actions* that you can take to get things done.
3. *Vote with Your Feet.* Make an instant work plan by allowing participants to choose the action they would most like to take part in.

Not Just an Exercise. More Like Learning by Doing.
You'll learn asset mapping by trying this. But the Quick and Simple Experience is not just a learning exercise. It's real and productive work for you and your congregation.

You will end up with specific, tangible actions that you can take to get things done. You will have people with the energy to act on those ideas!

What Will You Need?
- Paper (15-20 half-sheets per person)
- Thin markers
- Tape
- Clear wall space

1. **Recognize Your Assets**

Spend up to 20 minutes on this.

God has given us all gifts, that we can call strengths or assets. We start by recognizing and listing these assets.

Look at your half-full cup. The easiest, simplest, and fastest way to do this is to use the Reminder List of Basic Assets. Think about the five types of assets that you have:

> **Reminder List of Basic Assets**
> - Physical assets
> - Individual assets
> - Associations
> - Institutions
> - Economic assets

Remember, too, that the church is the people, and the people are the church. Your congregation has assets. As an individual, you have assets. Your individual assets are part of the mix. In asset mapping, we talk about both congregational and individual assets, equally and together.

Each person writes down assets they think of:
- Sit in small groups of four to eight people. Hand out the half-sheets of paper and the markers.
- Each person will generate a stack of assets by writing on these papers. Write each asset on a new sheet of paper. (Do not write a list of assets on one sheet.) Write in LARGE BLOCK LETTERS that everyone else can read from a distance.
- Write down specific assets in three of the four categories from the reminder list.
- Read your assets out loud to everyone in the group you are in.
- Tape the papers on the wall, in any order.

---

1. **Recognize Your Assets** (continued)

You are not trying to summarize the assets of your congregation. Nor can you expect to catalog all of your assets. The idea is to recognize and list assets that might be useful. You will want to dig deeper to remind yourself of assets you may have overlooked. Take two or three rounds, listing several assets in each category.

THOUGHT PROVOKERS

Use thought-provoking questions like these to jog your thinking about your assets. If time is limited, you do not need to cover all of the five types of Basic Assets. Try to recognize specific assets of a few types.

Choose three or more types of assets to work on.

Physical assets
- What are two or three physical assets of your congregation?
- What are other physical assets of your congregation that you would not have thought of at first? Think creatively! Be specific.

Individual assets
- What are one or two things you can do with your hands?
- What is something no one in church knows you care about?
- Name a few talents and skills of other people at your table.

Associations
- What groups of people do you connect with in your community? They can be inside or outside of the congregation.

Institutions
- What institutions have something in common with your congregation?

Economic assets
- What does your congregation spend money on?

Dig deeper
- What signs have you seen lately of God's grace in the world?

BE SPECIFIC
Not "the building" but "100 seats in the sanctuary."

BE CREATIVE
The most useful assets are often the weirdest or funniest ones.

2. Connect the Dots

Spend up to 20 minutes on this.

Development is creating a new link between two or more existing assets.

Forming Action Ideas from Assets
- Gather with your group by the wall and look over your assets.
- Think about God's will for your congregation, the gifts God has given you, and the actions you can take by using these gifts.
- As a group, brainstorm actions that connect two or more of these assets to accomplish God's will.

Contributing to Your Team
- Cluster the sheets of paper with the assets you have connected.
- Tell the others in your group what action you are thinking of.
- Other people can add assets to your cluster or start a new cluster. As you are clustering assets, talk to each other about the actions you might develop.

Naming Actions
- You want to end up with a few (two to six) clusters of assets representing particular actions you've discovered through brainstorming. Give each action a short name. Write that name down on another sheet and post it with the asset cluster.

**Action 1—
cluster of assets**

**Action 2—
cluster of assets**

**Action 3—
cluster of assets**

2. **Connect the Dots** (continued)

DO NOT put assets into categories based on similarity.

It is a common instinct to find likeness, but it can stop you from acting.

DO connect diverse assets to brainstorm ACTIONS.

> **Think about actions like:**
> - Project
> - Event
> - Performance
> - Campaign
> - Protest
> - Celebration
> - Demonstration
> - Making, growing, or fixing things

As you work together, feel free to write down more assets.

The same asset can be used more than once. Just write it down again on another sheet of paper.

3. Vote with Your Feet

This should take less than 10 minutes.

Follow Your Heart
- Listen to each group report on the actions they have discovered through brainstorming.
- Decide which of these actions you would most like to take part in yourself.
- Go stand next to that action.

You get an instant work plan
- The job before you
- The people with you, who have an interest in the same idea
- The assets you can connect to get things done

Now look around. What do you notice?

Learning by Doing

Questions to Consider and Discuss

Spend about 10 minutes on this.

Impressions
- Looking around the room at people standing by the assets clustered into actions on the wall, what do you observe?
- Did anything surprise you in the experience?

Sensing the power of faith in community
- How did it feel to write down your assets?
- How did it feel to connect the dots?
- How did it feel when you voted with your feet?

Recognizing results
- When you connected the dots, what kinds of actions emerged?
- Taken together, what would these actions accomplish?
- What have you accomplished already?

Thinking about open-sum dynamics
- How much faith is there in the world? If I get more faith, does it come out of your supply? Or does your faith strengthen mine, and my faith increase yours, and our faith grow on others?
- How many assets are there in our community? If we connect the dots, do we use up our assets? Do we create new assets to use more and more?

Using and sharing asset mapping
- Can you apply what you did to your daily life or to congregational life?
- Could you facilitate the Quick and Simple Congregational Asset-Mapping Experience with others?

Abundance

Affinity

Release

PART TWO

The HOW

How Do We Map Assets?

Now that you have a sense of *what* asset mapping is, you may have an idea about how you can apply asset mapping in your congregation. This part of the book will tell you more about *how* to do that.

This part of this the book provides detailed advice and guidance for facilitating the Quick and Simple Congregational Asset-Mapping Experience. This section addresses subjects such as how and when you might approach groups with the idea of asset mapping, how to easily facilitate a smooth process, and how to steer clear of dead ends. I also include sample focus questions and mini-exercises for particular situations. In the end, you will be able to tailor the Quick and Simple Congregational Asset-Mapping Experience to your own style and the practice of the group you are working with.

I've written this section in response to requests from people who have been through the Quick and Simple Experience and have been so inspired and impressed that they want to share the process with other groups. These requests come from clergy and laypeople who see asset mapping as a support to their calls in congregations and communities of faith.

Chapter 3

Basements, Halls, and Meeting Rooms

Opportunities Everywhere

ASSET MAPPING GENERATES new opportunities for faithful action. It's not a way of telling people what to do. It's a way of empowering people to do what their hearts tell them to do. Asset mapping isn't something you do *instead of* your current ways of getting things done; it's something you can do *in support of* your current ways of getting things done.

The Quick and Simple Asset-Mapping Experience is not a part of a formal planning system or a decision-making program; it's an experience in a way of

---

Asset mapping empowers people to do what their hearts tell them to do. It's a way of thinking and acting.

---

thinking and acting. It's a way to show participants that they *already know* how to see the half-full cup, connect the dots, and act on their faith.

WHO, ME?

You can facilitate asset mapping. You can do this even if you're "not good with groups."

You will find you can facilitate asset mapping because you've done it before— lots of times. Every time you saw the value of somebody's assets and connected them with someone else, you have been a facilitator. You have already facilitated asset mapping if you've ever:

- Connected a buyer to a seller
- Brought a dish to a congregational lunch
- Prayed with strangers
- Helped form a team or a league
- Bought things with others in bulk
- Told a story and listened to a story
- Helped raise money for a neighbor in crisis
- Joined a church
- Worked on a Habitat for Humanity house
- Started a small business
- Pitched in to strengthen your congregation

Anytime you've done any of these simple actions, you have helped people connect their own strengths, assets, and gifts to get something done. You've already facilitated asset mapping. Facilitating this Quick and Simple Asset-Mapping Experience will remind you of past successes and build your confidence for future action. This section will give you plenty of tips for facilitating this kind of experience with groups.

CONSULTANT'S JOURNAL

I used to think group success depended on my skill. Now I know better.
Over the years, my thinking about consulting and group facilitation has changed because of asset mapping. An important shift happened a few days after my visit with two congregations in North Carolina.

I've worked with many different groups over the years, starting when I was just a teenager. I've been "facilitated," and I've facilitated groups myself. I've thought hard about what makes groups work. Until recently, I would have said the success of the process depends on the skill of the facilitator. When a group works well together, I'd say it must have been because the facilitator did a good job. If a group does not work well, I would wonder what the facilitator could have done better.

Of course I'd also think about the particular group situation but usually as a kind of excuse. For example, I'd reason that an uncooperative participant disrupted one group or another group was unsure about its own goals. I'd try to learn from these things to do a better facilitation job next time.

As I have grown with this Quick and Simple Congregational Asset-Mapping Experience, however, something remarkable has happened. Now, groups always seem to work well together—when they are building on their assets. In every context and every group dynamic I've observed that people would come out of the asset-mapping experience smiling, laughing, and bursting with new energy. If one participant was negative, the group's positive energy would affirm that participant and draw the person into the circle.

If a group was uncertain or confused, the group would find mission and meaning in the connections between their gifts.

I felt great about my facilitation skills from all of this. But eventually I had to wonder. Nobody's that good. *There's something going on here, I thought, something bigger than me.*

Then I facilitated a congregational asset-mapping experience with the two congregations in North Carolina. A few days later, I called one of the pastors to see what he thought. He was very excited. The participants had grappled with tough issues in the context of using their gifts. They had come away with an action agenda that no one had thought possible. What's more, the connection of gifts and positive energy had already had miraculous results.

I was amazed by all of this good news. You see, there had been some delays in the proceedings, and I had a plane to catch. I had to leave before the asset mapping finished. At the time all of this came together for these people, I wasn't even in the room!

What made the asset-mapping experience click for these people? Obviously it wasn't just me. Something bigger was going on. I'm just a part of it, like you are, like we all are.

And you know, I feel great about this. You might think that as a consultant I'd feel somehow disappointed or threatened, that the group didn't need my skills and personal charm to get great results. Instead, I feel joy. It makes my heart glad to know I'm a part of a larger movement of faith and to feel the power of that movement. It makes me want to share what I've experienced with anyone I can reach.

Pass it along. Pay it forward. We're all part of something bigger.

With Whom?

Asset Mapping in Groups

Any group of people can do asset mapping together. I have seen it work with eight people in an office and with 1,000 people in a convention hall. I have seen it work with an excitable class of fourth graders and with a sedate senior's club. I have seen it work with rich people and poor people, professionals and working people, men and women, city people and country people, and people of all races. I have seen it work with people of all religions.

Even better, it works with a mix of people. I have seen groups from two competing congregations come together to do asset mapping. I have seen young people and older people connect the dots around a table as equals. I have seen ecumenical and interfaith groups use asset mapping to strengthen their faith and take action together. I have seen groups of people who had never met come together and, by doing asset mapping, become partners on immediate and tangible projects.

> **Asset mapping works with**
> - A mix of people
> - People you care about
> - Your entire congregation
> - Your church board
> - Committees
> - Bible study groups
> - Any group of faith

In asset mapping every person's assets go up on the wall together, everybody collaborates to connect the dots, and each person is free and able to follow his or her heart to accomplish the common good. In other words, everyone is included and respected. So, asset mapping works well with a mix of people. But more than that, asset mapping works well for bringing a mix of people together.

Instead of asking yourself, "With whom should I do asset mapping?" ask, "With whom do I want to grow stronger?" The important thing is that you facilitate asset mapping with people you care about. If you care about the people you work with on this, you will start from a position of respect. You will begin with some understanding of their gifts and interests. You will care about the outcome—not that a particular outcome is achieved, but that the participants experience success on their terms. You'll want to see that group grow stronger in mission together.

CONSULTANT'S JOURNAL

I share this with you because someone shared this with me.

I was only 18 when I first received and understood the gift of asset thinking from another faithful person. I was organizing tenants with a community organization in inner-city Chicago, on a summer internship funded by a grant from the Kennedy School of Government at Harvard. Tenants in one building reacted when the slumlord stopped paying his gas, water, and electric bills. The health and the lives of tenants were threatened. Together we organized a rent strike to force the slumlord to pay his bills.

Though it was the middle of the day, I saw yawns and tired looks on people's faces as they sat down at the fateful meeting, where they would decide whether to strike or not. The tenants joked with each other about this. I asked the tenant leader, Ms. Bryant, what was going on. She said that nobody had slept the night before, because they were worried about being evicted. Even though it was perfectly legal to withhold rent until the bills were paid, the tenants all knew that the slumlord was a powerful man who could punish them if he chose.

> *I asked Ms. Bryant how she and the others could find the courage to stand up against the slumlord. "This is your home," I said. "How can you risk so much?"*
>
> *She said to me, "This is our home. How can we afford not to?"*
>
> *Sometimes I look back on this moment with embarrassment at my naiveté, born of privilege. But Ms. Bryant's words rang in my heart and mind like a call. She transformed my focus from the risk of action to the risk of inaction. Where I worried about the power we didn't have, she appreciated the assets she did have—in her home and her neighbors. Instead of a half-empty cup, I suddenly saw a cup half full.*
>
> *The tenants did decide to strike. We won. The slumlord immediately paid his bills and restored basic services to the tenants. I learned how the transformation of the mind could bring together and empower a small group of people against all odds. I've been moved to share this lesson ever since. My affinity with people seeking change started the day Ms. Bryant showed me how to see the half-full cup.*

Once you experience the power of asset mapping, you'll want to share it. You will see a group of people who are stuck in negative thinking and you'll want to tell them, "You should do some asset mapping." And you'll probably be right. But that approach is not going to work for you as a facilitator.

Instead, you can share what you've learned by saying, "We should do asset mapping together." When you facilitate asset mapping, it's not about *them*. It has to be about *us*. It's your affinity with the group—not your expertise—that will make your facilitation successful. We'll discuss this further as we talk about how asset mapping leads to widening the circle of people we engage with. Because, as you'll discover, your affinity for the group you are working with is the beginning of a growing snowball of faith that motivates action, and action that motivates faith.

The Quick and Simple Congregational Asset-Mapping Experience is a group process, but asset mapping is driven by personal transformation. Each of us learns to see the half-full cup. We learn to recognize and appreciate our gifts, strengths, and assets instead of our needs or deficiencies. As we transform our thinking about our own gifts, we recognize that the value of those gifts comes from connecting them with the gifts of others. And that motivates us to work in groups.

Groups in Congregations

Each of us draws on personal faith. We seek to apply and strengthen our faith by making connections with other people. Congregations are communities of

27

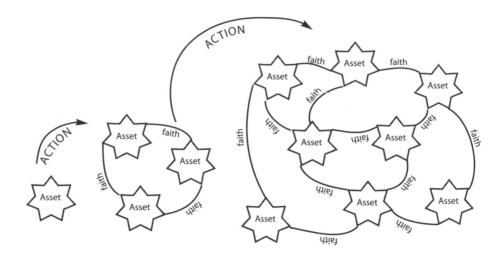

Figure 3A: Building on Assets Creates Snowballing Faith and Action

faith. It's only natural that we often start asset mapping in and among congregations.

I have worked with a variety of congregations of different denominations. For example, I have been staffing a project for the Evangelical Lutheran Church in America in which congregations develop their own approaches and uses for congregational asset mapping. Urban, rural, and suburban churches have participated. Each congregation has gone about asset mapping differ-

Your affinity for the group you are working with
is the beginning of a growing snowball
of faith that motivates action, and
action that motivates faith.

ently, pulling in different groups and making their own plans as appropriate to their situation. And from this local context, each has experienced the power of looking at the half-full cup and connecting the dots. Here are some examples of groups in congregations that could do asset mapping with you.

- **A gathering open to the whole congregation**
  The entire congregation can do asset mapping. Often, congregations will hold an asset-mapping session right after worship services and open the event to anyone who wants to come.
- **Leadership and governing councils**
  Church boards and other governing bodies frequently use asset mapping as a tool for planning.

- **Standing committees**
  As we'll discuss in this book, asset mapping has particular relevance and value to diverse standing committees of congregations, with missions ranging from stewardship to social justice, from property maintenance to building campaigns. These committees use asset mapping to strengthen their mission and increase their effectiveness.

- **Bible study groups and religious education classes**
  The Quick and Simple Asset-Mapping Experience provides a vivid object lesson for Bible study and religious education. Groups use asset mapping both to illustrate aspects of religious teaching and to put those teachings into action. Participants ask questions like, "How did the people in this Bible passage see the fullness of God's grace (or not!)? And how did they put God's gifts to work to get things done?" In this ongoing discussion, the asset-mapping experience helps show us how those Bible stories are real and present for us in daily life.

---

*Asset mapping transforms the way
we look at the world.*

- **Interest groups, discussion groups, and social groups**
  Adult and youth groups like to try asset mapping in an informal way at their regular meetings. This works whenever people come together around common interests, from a women's circle to a youth group, from the men's breakfast to a cancer survivor meeting. These groups often use asset mapping to energize discussion, uncover participant's passions and interests, and open up participation.

- **Benevolent and fraternal groups, associated foundations, and special entities**
  Often there are formally organized groups in or around a congregation with special purposes like managing funds or property. These groups use asset mapping to plan and take action in a manner that strengthens their faithful association.

- **Partnerships, collaborations, and coalitions**
  Congregations often work in partnership with other groups or organizations. Sometimes congregations form peer-to-peer partnerships with other congregations in their own community or mission partnerships with congregations in another part of the world. Increasingly, rural churches are coming together to share resources in creative ways. For years, congregations have formed coalitions and collaborations for community organizing, public leadership, and other targeted action. Asset mapping is amazingly helpful for these partnerships, because it

enables each partner to identify what it brings to the table as a peer and equal. At the same time, asset mapping helps clarify and highlight how the combined contributions can add up to something bigger than any of the partners.

- **Any group of faith**
  You can think of other groups you care about in and around your own congregation. Use the Quick and Simple Experience any time you think it might help to focus on God's gifts, to get unstuck, and to create a snowball of faith and action.

- **Groups in public and personal life**
  Not all ministry happens in congregations. Our spiritual life does not start or end in a church or a temple. We witness to our faith in our daily lives as we lead our lives faithfully with others. So every group is a potential group for asset mapping.

Asset thinking will lead you to engage with wider circles of people even if you don't plan on that happening. All of the congregations I have worked with around asset mapping have come to see themselves as churches without walls. They see the community in the church and the church in the community. After asset mapping with a congregation, I've had participants say to me, "Hey, I'm going to try this with the board I serve on at the social service agency," or, "This would really help with the people I work with," and even, "I should share this with my family."

The more you practice asset thinking in a faith context, the more you understand how asset mapping can be a powerful and effective way to share your faith with others in your personal and public life. As you make your own path, every context can become a faith context.

Asset mapping provides a way for you to share your faith outside your congregation.

CONSULTANT'S JOURNAL

Sometimes we learn from children.

My son's fourth-grade class invited me to visit them for a unit they were doing on community planning. Instead of lecturing, I facilitated an asset-mapping exercise to show them two ways of planning. First, I asked the students to think of their needs and wrote these on the board. One student said that he needed a bigger bedroom. Another said that she needed a whole bedroom of her own. So a third student said that he needed a whole mansion. I asked the students how they could get these things. "Win the lottery," was the best answer.

Second, I asked the students to list some of their assets. We wrote down their individual talents, their books, clothing, the supplies and decorations in the classroom, even parts of the building itself.

Then I asked the students what they could do if they combined some of those assets in new ways. They came up with amazing ideas, connected with each other in fun new ways, and ended up with a list of actions they could start on immediately.

I came away from this learning as much, if not more, than the fourth graders. They taught me that any group could do asset mapping. They taught me that graceful experience doesn't have to happen in a church or a temple. And they taught me something about approaching faith with the mind of a child.

When Can I Put Asset Mapping in Action?

You can facilitate the Quick and Simple Experience with a group in almost any circumstance if the group is interested and willing to participate. Still, particular circumstances do come up that provide you with opportunities to act. Here are some of the circumstances where I have seen groups make good use of asset mapping.

- **When we gather with new people**
  You could suggest asset mapping as an excellent icebreaker and momentum starter for a group of people who are newly gathered. I have seen church councils use asset mapping after the election of new members, both to get to know each other and to take action on an emerging agenda. New groups forming around projects like a building campaign have used asset mapping to brainstorm strategy and create a spark.

  Two churches in rural northeast Iowa used asset mapping for their yoking process, as they joined together to share staff and other resources.

Use asset mapping
- When meeting with new people
- To renew an existing group
- To launch a campaign
- When planning
- In a crisis
- When reaching out
- To form partnerships
- In worship
- To get unstuck from conflict, neediness, or negativism

In that case, Pastor Bruce Hanson thought that the asset mapping was especially useful as a kind of second step. After the two congregations had gotten to know each other, they did asset mapping together over dinner after worship services. Asset mapping helped both congregations to identify their own strengths, to appreciate what they stood to gain from their partnership with each other, and to take action.

- **When we renew an existing group**
Some congregation groups that have been around a long time have used asset mapping to give themselves a boost. In that case, asset mapping works to spark creativity. Asset mapping helps groups get unstuck by shining a light on overlooked assets and by showing how those assets can be connected to get things done.

    Over the years, a stewardship committee in a congregation ended up focusing solely on an annual fundraising appeal. Asset mapping helped the committee and the congregation to see stewardship as something bigger, as their call to put all of God's gifts in action. A social justice committee in another congregation thought that they reached the same small group of people for every campaign or issue. Asset mapping helped these participants connect the dots to the things people cared about. The process involved more people and led to new advocacy and partnership development that built on their particular strengths.

- **When we campaign**
Congregations use campaigns such as building campaigns, stewardship campaigns, or hunger campaigns to drive toward larger goals. Campaigns are supposed to snowball; that is, they are supposed to involve more people over time. Asset mapping can create a spark for new faith and action. It's a perfect tool for starting or advancing a campaign.

    The members of one congregation talked and talked about starting a building campaign. Folks just could not imagine where the money would come from. But when a group of people did asset mapping on their own, they realized that the church property was a scarce and valuable location for a number of related community and nonprofit organizations. From a few discussions with those organizations, they developed ideas for sharing space and cost, and suddenly the campaign was off and running.

- **When we plan**
From time to time, congregation councils, boards, committees, and leaders will step back from the daily business to plan. That's an opportunity for asset mapping.

If you have ever been involved with strategic planning for your congregation, community, or voluntary organization, you may have experienced the frustration of working hard on a plan that then sits on a shelf.

Asset mapping cures that. Asset mapping puts action first, so it engages people right away. Asset mapping affirms the worth of each person's gifts, so the process is owned and is used by participants. Asset mapping helps people find affinity with each other by connecting the dots, so that more and more people get involved instead of fewer and fewer. Asset mapping builds on interests and affinities, in an open-sum way, so that no one feels rejected. Asset mapping does not pretend to reach a final solution or allocation of resources, so it avoids conflict. The point of asset mapping isn't any document, but action, so it cannot sit on a shelf.

In one congregation, the council used the Quick and Simple Congregational Asset-Mapping Experience as a substitute for traditional planning. In another, members of the congregation used asset mapping in conjunction with other kinds of planning to spark energy, creativity, and participation.

- **When there is a crisis**
Every congregation faces a crisis sooner or later. Sometimes these come from threats to the congregation's existence, over things like money, property, or doctrine. Other times these crises come in the form of threats to a congregation's members or to the broader community.

Asset mapping isn't a formal system of conflict resolution, counseling, fundraising, or mediation. But it can help with any of these things by focusing people on positive, collaborative action, as we will see in this book. A crisis always points to something that people care about, which is an asset. In fact, sometimes it takes a crisis for people to recognize the value of an asset that's been taken for granted. Asset mapping helps a community connect the dots between that asset and other assets to make good things happen.

A rural congregation had never been involved in local economic development before one member family lost their farm. The congregation built on assets to find ways to create jobs and economic opportunities in the community and to raise their voices for positive rural public policies.

- **When we reach out**
Every congregation is dedicated to sharing its faith. Even a growing congregation is constantly looking for ways to reach out to new members. And often a congregation will become settled with a core group of

people until they wake up one day and realize that they have lost membership and stand to lose even more if they do not act. This is a good chance for some asset mapping even if you don't call it outreach.

The education committee of a suburban congregation started asset mapping to identify and mobilize assets for teaching and learning. They ended up sponsoring an after-school project, which became a larger, midweek program at the church. This resulted in dozens of new confirmations and memberships from the people who were welcomed and attracted.

- **When we are partners**

  Whenever a congregation forms a partnership, there's an opportunity for asset mapping. The questions in partnerships are always, "What does each partner bring to the table and what does each partner take away?" Asset mapping specifically answers these questions so that each partner can imagine the larger good that comes from working together. The trick to partnerships is focusing on that larger good and not on the relative weakness of one partner to another.

  For example, five congregations in one rural area decided to form a partnership. They had in mind things like sharing pastoral staff and combining youth groups. Two of the congregations had larger memberships than the other three. But all of the congregations realized that the partnership would not hold up if it seemed that those two congregations were dominating. Using asset mapping, they identified gifts and strengths of each congregation. They found that the smaller congregations had many strengths, like a fully active membership and a broad geographical community. By connecting all of their gifts, the church partners came up with creative new projects and actions that they could not do on their own but that they could do together.

- **When we worship and pray**

  Asset mapping has a deep affinity with worship and prayer. Every time we come together to worship or pray as a congregation, we are building on our assets. We are doing something together that we could not do on our own. We are creating something larger than the sum of its parts.

  Asset mapping can start from the pulpit! In fact, it has already. If you preach, or if you listen to preaching, you've considered the abundance of God's gifts, our connections with each other as God's children, and how to love our neighbors. In worship and prayer, you've reflected on transforming your minds, placing your faith in God, acting on God's calling, and witnessing your faith to one other. Asset mapping is about reflecting and acting on these powerful things.

On the one hand, preachers can use the lessons of faith to help a congregation understand and use congregational asset mapping. On the other hand, preachers can apply the experience of asset mapping to help a congregation understand and use lessons of faith. The connection works both ways. Preachers can use asset mapping to exemplify connections between faith and life.

Down from the pulpit, we can reflect on the lessons of asset mapping in prayer and in Bible study. We can use asset mapping as a way to share our faith story in our daily lives. Asset mapping is a way we can strengthen our faith in action together, renewing our mission from and for congregation.

One pastor told me that she had been trying to preach and teach about abundance in her congregation for years. Then in one hour, when the congregation went through the Quick and Simple Congregational Asset-Mapping Experience together, she saw the light bulbs go on in the eyes of her people. The people appreciated gifts they'd overlooked and saw how they could use them together. Afterward one person said to her, "Now I get what you've been telling us all along." She responded that it was she who had learned from the congregation. That night she said grace at the dinner table with a renewed sense of appreciation and hope.

CONSULTANT'S JOURNAL

Something big is in the room.

Early in the national project we developed to test asset mapping in various congregational settings, I was invited to visit with a series of congregations around the country. The leaders asked me to talk to their congregations about asset mapping at worship services. Since I'm not a pastor or a theologian, I didn't feel comfortable giving a sermon from the pulpit, but I agreed to give temple talks at each congregation.

At the first service, I took my seat in a front pew and participated in the worship with everyone else. I had asset mapping on my mind as I followed the readings and the sermon. When I got up to give my temple talk, I thought to myself, "Wow. The readings and the sermon go really well with what I have to say to people about the half-full cup and connecting the dots. What a nice lead-in to my presentation."

Again at the next service, I listened to the lessons with asset mapping on my mind. Even though the texts were completely different, it seemed again that what I had to say about asset mapping would reinforce and extend the lessons of the day. I thought, "What a coincidence."

A third time it happened. The Old and New Testament readings and the sermon seemed to illustrate and to draw practical relevance from the asset-mapping messages of abundance, connection, and open-ended faith. This time I thought, "Wait a minute. There's something going on here, something bigger than me."

Maybe I'm projecting. They say that if all you have is a hammer, you'll see every problem as a nail. I could easily be guilty of that. But I don't think so. Instead, it's like getting a hammer when all I had was a sponge. What a wonder it is to see what all those nails have been about! I think there's something about asset mapping that fits with, illustrates, and explains the lessons of faith.

There's real power in the half-full cup, in the affinity we find when we connect our gifts, and in the openness we achieve when we build on assets. When I experience the results of asset mapping, it feels like something big is in the room.

How Do I Introduce the Idea to a Group?

So you have an affinity with a group of people. You sense an opportunity to facilitate asset mapping with that group. How do you approach the subject with the group? What's the pitch? It's easy. Just remember what asset mapping is and is not.

- **Asset mapping is supportive.**
  Asset mapping isn't some formal program to take the place of the group's way of getting things done. You don't want to say, "Hey, I want you to stop doing things that way and try this great new system I found out about." Instead, asset mapping is a way of thinking that the group can use to extend and strengthen its ministry. It's not *instead of* what you are already doing. It *supports* what you are doing that builds faith and community.

  The Quick and Simple Asset-Mapping Experience contains steps and procedures that a group can follow to make it easier for participants to experience asset thinking. But it's not meant to be a formal program. It demonstrates a way of thinking and acting even as it results in practical and immediate benefits. Sooner or later, participants will get the idea

---

Asset mapping is
- Supportive
- Familiar
- A snowball
- Free
- Part of a larger movement

---

and apply asset thinking all the time, without steps or pieces of paper on a wall. The Quick and Simple Experience can spread that around and speed up the snowball effect.

You might say something like this: "We did a lot of good work on our plans for this year and we've all gotten behind the new campaign. I know a lot of us are wondering how we are going to get all this done, and especially how we are going to engage people in our congregation. I've been looking at some different approaches to church development that seem to go together and fit with our faith and direction. One quick and easy process we could try is called congregational asset mapping."

- **It's familiar.**

Second, remember that asset thinking isn't really new to any of these groups in and around the congregation. These groups have all been connecting their gifts with faith from the beginning.

Has the congregation ever held a potluck supper, a pitch-in lunch, or a covered-dish dinner? (We call it by different names in different places.) Then people have identified some of their assets and connected them to participate in something bigger. Or, consider how we worship together and make a temple to God.

Your opportunity to do asset mapping with a group in the congregation is really an opportunity to demonstrate this existing asset thinking, celebrate it, and do it some more. You might say something like: "It was great how the whole congregation responded when the Gomez family lost their home in that fire. It reminds me of how many wonderful and faithful people we have in this community and how much we can get done when we work together. We can apply same kind of spirit to our goals as a congregation. That's basically what congregational asset mapping is for."

- **It snowballs.**

Third, congregational asset mapping is a way to create a snowball of faith and action around your congregation. Snowballing is the way I describe a pattern of self-reinforcing growth that builds on itself, getting bigger and bigger over time. With asset mapping, we act on our faith, which strengthens our faith to act some more. Asset mapping models how faith grows in community.

You might say something like: "We don't just want to start a new program or project. What we really want to do is spread our faith. We want to share the joy we experience with others. We want to build momentum. The way to do that is by starting with thanksgiving for the abundant gifts we have received from God. When we see our half-full cup, we'll see how to connect our gifts to make good things happen. And that will start a snowball of faith and action around the congregation."

- **It's free.**

  To top it off, the Quick and Simple Experience costs little or nothing to try. All it takes is an hour or so of time, pens, paper, and tape. If nothing else, it breaks the ice, builds relationships, and provides a way to brainstorm ideas. You can be sure of gaining new perspective. And if (when!) asset mapping does lead to a snowball of faith and action, amazing things can happen. There's very little downside to asset mapping—and a lot of upside.

  You might say something like: "Since we've got new people in our group now, it's a good chance for us to get to know each other and start the ball rolling on some new plans. I suggest we use congregational asset mapping to take at look at our strengths and how we can use them to accomplish our mission together. It only takes an hour. We ought to get to know each other anyway."

- **It's part of a larger movement.**

  Don't be surprised if other people in the group say they've heard of asset mapping or have done something with it before. There's something of a movement afoot, and asset mapping is right in the middle of that movement.

  People who promote community health have been using asset strategies for years now. So have youth workers, community development corporations, and activists in rural and inner-city areas. The pioneering book of asset-based community development (ABCD), *Building Communities from the Inside Out: A Path toward Finding and Mobilizing a Community's Assets* by John McKnight and Jody Kretzmann, two community activists and thinkers, is said to be the best-selling book in community-development history, even without a major publisher. Word about asset mapping has passed from friend to friend, colleague to colleague.

  ABCD has been connected with many faith traditions for some time. Networks of people are applying and adapting asset methods in many denominations, large and small. Sometimes these networks have formed around church development, sometimes around specific ministries. Sometimes the approach has come from international mission work or Habitat for Humanity. Other times it has spread through networks in stewardship, evangelism, and worship.

  In spirit and approach, asset mapping complements and connects with other emerging ways of looking at social development and spiritual leadership, approaches such as abundance theory, servant leadership, or appreciative inquiry. People in your group might note these connections and many more. All the better. Welcome those connections, because they are in harmony with the larger movement.

And finally, don't be surprised if members of your group want to take the congregational asset mapping ideas and methods back to other groups they belong to. That's how the movement spreads. The more we build on our gifts, the more gifts we have to build on.

How Do I Get Ready to Lead a Group?

When you've got a group of people you want to do asset mapping with, you're ready to set the time and place for the session. What's great about the Quick and Simple Congregational Asset-Mapping Experience is that it's quick, simple, and doesn't require any fancy equipment or formal space. All it takes is a large room, pens, paper, tape, and an hour or so of everybody's time.

The experience will go more smoothly if you get things ready ahead of time. Here's a little more detail about the logistics to help you get ready to lead a group in asset mapping.

- **Blank walls**
  You'll be sticking pieces of paper on the wall and moving them around, so a room with plain walls—no fancy wallpaper or art—work best. Often, church basements, fellowship halls, or classrooms make excellent space. If you don't have a room with plain blank walls, you can improvise. Attach asset papers to room dividers, windows, or doors. You can cover walls with a bedsheet. I've seen people put their asset papers on the floor. My colleague Bob Sitze told me that one time he attached poster boards from the ceiling!

- **Tables and chairs**
  Set up the room with enough tables and chairs for your participants to sit in groups of four to eight people. Don't put the chairs in rows facing

---

To do asset mapping you need
- A large room with blank walls
- Tables and chairs for groups of four to eight people
- 10 or 15 half-sheets (5½″ x 8½″) of paper per person
- One thin marking pen per person
- One roll of masking tape per table
- Optional: flip chart

---

the front—this isn't a speech or a presentation. Groups sitting around tables work best for sharing assets.

- **Paper**
  Each person should have 10 or 15 sheets of paper. In my experience, the best paper is 8½ x 11 copier paper cut in half. You can cut these yourself. You can also buy pads of paper this size.

- **Thin markers**
  Each participant will be reading the asset papers on a wall. The writing should be visible. Thin markers write dark enough to be seen and fine enough to make words legible.

- **Masking tape**
  Each group of four to eight participants will use masking tape to attach their asset papers to the wall. Give each group their own roll. To speed things along, you can tear little strips of tape beforehand. Or, at that point in the exercise, this can be the job of one person in the group.

  Sticky notepaper does not work for this. The paper is designed to be not so sticky. The pieces of paper fall off the wall and distract the group from the process. They aren't usually available in large enough sizes. I have seen professional facilitators spray a large sheet of flip-chart paper and then smaller sheets of ordinary paper will stick to the sheet.

- **Optional: flip chart**
  A flip chart is useful for recording participants' contributions at the end of the experience.

How Will We Use Our Time?

As indicated, the Quick and Simple Congregational Asset-Mapping Experience can be done in about an hour, which is broken down like this:

Asset Mapping Agenda	
20 minutes	1. Recognizing Our Assets
20 minutes	2. Connecting the Dots
10 minutes	3. Voting with Our Feet
10 minutes	4. Reflecting on What Happened

If you have more or less than an hour to work with, Recognizing Our Assets is the most flexible step. The more assets you identify, the more you learn to see God's abundance. You could devote anywhere from 10 minutes to half hour to the first part.

Connecting the Dots is a group process that has more to do with the group dynamics than your role as a facilitator. Sometimes groups take off right away. More often, there is a sort of learning curve for participants that starts slowly and then suddenly comes together in a rush. If you cut this short, you may miss the rush. You might leave a little extra time just in case it is needed.

The third step, Voting with Our Feet, is fast, easy, and fun. Larger gatherings can and should shorten their group report period. You'll want time at the end to look around at what you see.

That's the end of the asset-mapping process, but don't leave yet. We're trying to start a cycle of learning by doing and acting from faith. So take this opportunity, while your group is together, to begin reflecting on what you've learned from the action of asset mapping. Ten minutes is enough to capture your immediate observations while they are fresh. This short reflection will start the ball rolling for continued reflection.

If you have a little longer than an hour, 90 minutes works for a nice, full session. The extra time allows people to uncover more assets and make creative connections. If you don't have a full hour, you may be able to squeeze this particular process into 50 minutes.

If you try to do something even faster than 50 minutes, I think you'll end up cutting one or two of the steps. You could simply brainstorm assets, like listing all of the community associations people can think of. Or you could cut out brainstorming the assets, jump to brainstorming actions, then voting with your feet. Clearly, these versions lose something significant, but they could be helpful to a group just trying to get an idea of what asset mapping is all about.

Asset mapping can also be done as part of longer event, such as a half-day, full-day, or two-day retreat. But I wouldn't spend more than 90 minutes on the process itself. Instead, I would invest that time in discussion and mutual learning to start that snowball of faith and action. I would even do a Quick and Simple Experience again, with a different focus. I would also concentrate on opportunities for sharing the idea and the process with others.

Try It and See!

The Quick and Simple Congregational Asset-Mapping Experience is a wonderful taste of the power of faith and community. But nothing replaces the actual experience. Why not try it and see?

Asset mapping will make you act,
smile, and wonder.

It's fun! It's uplifting! You'll smile as you recognize and affirm each other's gifts. You'll wonder at the way new actions and ideas arise from those assets. You'll feel empowered by the freedom you gain to follow your heart. And you'll be amazed at the larger mission that emerges from collective efforts of people working together in faith.

Chapter 4

Before Step One

An Optional Jumping-Off Point

Most groups want to start right off with asset mapping, and that's great. But for some groups in some congregations, I've found an opening preamble that is useful to the experience.

What Happens

CENTERING
Participants prepare for asset mapping by asking themselves, "What is God's will for this community?"

The Facilitator's Task

As facilitator, you simply ask the question and write down people's responses on a flip chart or blackboard.

The Process

After introductions and prayer, open up the Congregational Asset-Mapping Experience with this question, "What is God's will for this community?" Go around the room or open the floor for people to say whatever comes from their heart. If you like, you can write the responses on a flip chart.

STEERING CLEAR OF DEAD ENDS

This isn't a question for discussion. Allow people to call out their gut responses, and then move to Step One: Recognizing Our Assets.

KEYS FOR NOTICING GOD'S WILL

When I ask, "What is God's will for your community?" I've been amazed by the responses. Sometimes people are down-to-earth, listing specific advancements that could be made in the community. Other times people are spiritual, even quoting from the Bible. And sometimes there's a fascinating mix of answers. All answers are good answers. The experience of asset mapping will show how the spiritual and the practical answers are all part of our collective witness to God's grace.

This opening is especially useful for groups that aren't organized around any specific task or goal, or for people who feel stuck in their situation.

THE MAIN THING TO REMEMBER

The Optional Jumping-Off Point is a way to focus people on their faith in community before they start asset mapping. What you write down on the flip chart isn't as important as the time participants spend thinking about the question of God's will in their community.

Use this option for focusing groups on mission.
People who chose the Optional Jumping-off Point opening say it laid a foundation of spiritual contemplation. At the same time, this start seems to help participants focus their thinking on faithful witness and action. For that reason, this beginning is especially useful for groups that aren't organized around any specific task or goal. It also helps with people who feel stuck in their situation. Either way, their responses will come to mind later, as participants brainstorm ways to connect assets to get things done.

CONSULTANT'S JOURNAL

No one ever asked before.

One pastor said that this opening was the most important part of the experience for him. "No one ever asked us to name God's will for this community," he said. "And we never asked ourselves, either. We've tended to focus on the immediacies of daily life, and the spiritual in general, and the survival of our congregation. This opened me up to a new way of thinking."

Chapter 5

Step One

Recognizing Our Assets

> **ABUNDANCE**
> We transform our thinking from the mind-set of deficiency to the mind-set of abundance, from seeing the cup half empty to seeing the cup half full. We recognize and appreciate the abundant gifts we have received and can use for faithful witness in our lives.

Recognizing Our Assets is fun and exciting. Participants react immediately and positively to the idea of looking at assets instead of needs. Naming assets clicks with both our faith and our world outlook.

We live in a society that surrounds us with a need-based, fixed-sum way of thinking and acting. We have developed personal strategies and approaches, competing with each other over supposedly fixed resources. We play the scarcity game even though we know that we are blessed with many gifts.

When we recognize and appreciate our assets, we transform our thinking. Instead of seeing needs and deficiencies, we see gifts and strengths. We transform negatives into positives. We see our cup as half full.

This transformation does not happen because the facilitator says it should. It works by experience, and we learn by doing. People are transformed by experiencing asset mapping. We learn to focus on assets by doing it. The first step of the Quick and Simple Congregational Asset-Mapping Experience uses focus questions and group affirmation to help participants remember and appreciate our blessings. However, the asset-mapping process does not invent something new. We find the thankful, asset-based perspective that exists within each of us. The experience of recognizing assets reminds us of what we already know.

We seem to recognize our assets under *layers* of thinking. That is, we dig through layer after layer of negative assumptions, attitudes, and beliefs to find the gifts we already know. The process outlined in this book works in stages or rounds, posing consecutively deeper questions to reveal overlooked assets.

Like peeling back the layers of an onion, participants recognize and appreciate set after set of assets. We start with gifts that are immediately obvious. From there, we uncover another layer of assets that were not so obvious at first. We dig deeper. We think bigger. We turn needs inside out. We widen our circle of attention.

When we do this, at some point we look up and say to ourselves, "Wow! Look at all these gifts!" The discovery of layer upon layer of blessings transforms our thinking. The *fullness* of God's grace suddenly becomes obvious to us.

The Facilitator's Task

As facilitator, your job is to lead the participants in stages or rounds of asset identification. You can use any of a number of thought provoking questions and prompts to move participants along. But, in the end, what matters is not the questions, how you ask them, or how many assets participants identify. In the end, what matters are the layers of perspective that participants dig through. This process transforms the thinking of the participants. Instead of seeing only scarcity, now they can see abundance!

The Process

Review the guide to the Quick and Simple Congregational Asset-Mapping Experience in chapter 2. It's enough for you to facilitate the process of asset mapping. Read this section for more detailed suggestions on the process and a list of useful focus questions.

Opening Directions

Make sure each participant has 10 or 15 half-sheets of paper and a thin marker (see How Do I Get Ready to Lead a Group in chapter 3, above). Make sure there is room in the center of each table for a large pile of asset papers.

Hold up a piece of blank paper. Tell participants that each sheet of paper is for one asset. The papers are not for writing lists. Each asset goes on a single sheet of paper.

Remind participants to write clearly and legibly so that others can read their assets when they are taped to the wall. I usually pick up a piece of paper myself and write "LARGE BLOCK LETTERS" on it to show people what I mean. Then I ask someone further away from me if they can read what I wrote.

> **CONSULTANT'S JOURNAL**
> ***Can everybody see this?***
> *I held up a sheet with LARGE BLOCK LETTERS written on it, and asked if every-one could see it. The group of youth and youth developers were still pretty quiet. I asked again, louder, "Can everybody see this writing?" A pastor in the back called out, "No!" I was ready to respond about the importance of legible writing, but everyone else was laughing. I looked around, lost. Finally some-body clued me in to the joke. "The pastor is blind," they explained.*
>
> *Later I worked with the pastor's small group on Connecting the Dots, mak-ing sure that everyone spoke the names of the assets out loud as they moved them around. The pastor said to the group, "What I really appreciate about this process is how visual it is, with all the assets up on the wall at once." The amazing thing is, he meant it.*

It doesn't matter how many assets people write down in response to any question. They cannot write too few or too many. Suggest "a few." Each partic-ipant writes down some assets, they read them *out loud* to the others at the table, as they toss them into the pile in the center.

Get right into it and soon everyone will get the hang of it. Pick a thought provoking asset question from the ones in the list below. Ask participants to write down a few assets that come to mind in response to that question. For example, you might start with, "Name a few physical assets of our church."

Walk-Around Facilitation

Walk around while people are writing down their assets. Remind people to read them out loud and toss them into the pot.

After a little while, get everyone's attention. Ask a second focus question. Often the best second question is the same as the first question, only more detailed. Ask something like, "Think deeper. What's an answer to the first ques-tion that you wouldn't have thought of at first?" Tell participants to be as specific and detailed as possible. You are not asking them to summarize their assets. You are not asking that they paint an accurate profile. You are just trying to get them to remember things of possible value to them.

After you think participants have had enough time to do this, pick another thought-provoking focus question, and then another, leading participants through several rounds of recognizing and sharing assets with each other.

Try This: Demonstrate a Specific Response.
Find an asset paper someone has completed with a very general response. For the physical assets question, a common general asset might be "the church." Read that out loud to the group. Then ask for more specific answers like the sanctuary, the chairs in the sanctuary, or even better, 100 Bibles.

Finishing

In the one-hour timetable, you should give this part about 15 or 20 minutes. People will probably be getting into their group process and may not want to stop. You could spend more time on Recognizing Our Assets if you have it.

But, sooner or later, you'll have to interrupt everyone and call an end to this part of the experience. That's okay. There will be plenty of opportunities for people to recognize assets in the time ahead. In fact, people usually grow and develop over time as they think about the half-full cup in their daily lives. Right now, we're looking to plant that seed, not to grow the whole forest.

Move right into the next part, Connect the Dots, without a break.

Choosing Your Focus Questions

In a one-hour Quick and Simple Experience, you'll spend up to 20 minutes on Recognizing Our Assets. You will have time to ask up to 10 focus questions. Start with the sample questions provided in the Quick and Simple Guide. You can't go wrong with those questions.

For your particular group, you may want to choose alternative focus questions. Or, after you've done this once, you might try something different the next time. That's fine. Personally, I vary the questions I use, depending on the situation and the people involved. Remember, it's really the rounds of questions that make this work, not so much the questions themselves. So go ahead and have fun with it. Make up your own questions or try others from this list.

> **Follow your own experience**
> This list of useful focus questions springs from the same ideas you used in the Personal Asset Starter in chapter 1. Review your own answers in the Personal Asset Starter. Think about what worked for you and why. Keep your own experience in mind as you choose questions to use as a facilitator. That will help you identify with the participants as you facilitate.

Sample Thought-Provoking Focus Questions
for Recognizing Assets

These are sample asset questions for you to choose from. Try up to 10 that might be interesting for a particular group.

First-glance questions. My favorite starting point for brainstorming our assets comes from asset pioneers John McKnight and Jody Kretzmann. They suggest five basic types of community assets, not to categorize assets, but to spark our thinking about all of the gifts we have. I like these basic types because they are easy to understand. In addition, they do not push people into the typical categories we use around congregations and communities.

Here are the five types, and some questions you could use to encourage people to recognize these assets. There's no particular rank or order to these. I have listed the easiest ones first because they work best for getting started. If time is short, I'd drop the last one or two categories—institutional and economic assets.

1. **Physical assets**
   Physical assets are things you can touch, see, or feel. These include land and natural resources, buildings and space, equipment, materials, and objects. People also sometimes think of strengths like location and visibility in response to these questions.

McKnight and Kretzmann's Five Basic Types of Community Assets
1. Physical assets
2. Individual assets
3. Associations
4. Institutions
5. Economic assets

- What are some physical assets of our congregation?
- Think deeper: what are some very specific assets of our congregation?
- What are some physical assets that are unique to our congregation?
- What are some physical assets of our community?
- What are some of our natural resources?

2. **Individual assets.**

   These are the talents, experience, perspective, and skills of individuals.
   - What are some things you care a lot about? (Gifts of the Heart)
   - What is something you know a lot about? (Gifts of the Head)
   - What's something you can do with your hands or body? (Gifts of the Hands)

   Sometimes people are shy about naming their gifts, or just don't see them. If people know at least one other person at their table, you could ask:
   - What are some talents or skills you see in someone else at your table?
   - What are some talents or skills you see in someone you know, who isn't here?

   To dig a little deeper, you could ask:
   - What talent or skill do you think people in the congregation or group know you for?
   - What's something you can do that people in the congregation don't even know about?

3. **Associations**

   These are voluntary groups, associations, networks, and organizations of individuals who gather to do or enjoy something together that they could not experience on their own. They might be more formal groups with a name, or they could be informal groups like the people who have coffee on Tuesdays at the café.
   - What are some groups of people you get together with from the congregation?
   - What groups or associations are you part of outside the congregation?
   - What are some groups you know about but are not a part of?
   - What are some groups that are not represented here?
   - Who's the most famous or powerful person you know?

4. **Institutions**

   These are business firms, public agencies, and nonprofit institutions with budgets, staff, and usually, places of business. Institutions differ from voluntary associations in the motivation of participants. People generally participate in institutional activities because of salaries, sales, taxes, or other financial or legal considerations.

- What are some institutional decisions that affect the people in the congregation and community? Which institutions make those decisions?
- What are some institutions represented in the congregation?
- What institutions does the congregation itself partner with or do business with?
- What institutions have something in common with the congregation?

5. **Economic assets**

Usually people think of local businesses as economic assets. We should also think of our spending power, our investing power, and our productive capacity to provide valuable goods or services.

- What's something the congregation spends money on?
- What's something you spend money on?
- What's something you can make or do, that people would pay you for?
- What businesses are represented in the congregation?
- Where does the congregation invest its money?
- What space does the congregation control that could be rented or charged for?

Second-glance questions. The following questions are designed to help participant's think outside of the box. They work by association—each question will unlock different thoughts for different people. Bear in mind, then, that any one of these questions could be very useful to one person but not to another. Choose one or two categories to use in a single session.

1. **Open up.**

The five types of community assets share a concrete, down-to-earth quality. Everyone can easily understand and engage with the categories. That's a good starting point, and that may be appropriate for a secular community context. But in a community of faith we want to open ourselves up to a spiritual perspective.

> Second-glance Questions
> 1. Open up.
> 2. Dig deeper.
> 3. Think bigger.

I mentioned earlier how Bishop Mark Hanson of the Evangelical Lutheran Church of America tells about the agenda of his church council when he was a parish pastor (*Faithful yet Changing: The Church in Challenging Times* [Augsburg Books, 2002]). They would open every council meeting by going around the table and asking each other,

"What signs have you seen of God's grace?"

I couldn't suggest a better asset question to encourage people to open up to the gifts of the divine.

2. **Dig deeper.**

There are so many gifts and assets. Why are some assets missed? Often it's because the assets are either too close or too far away.

We sometimes take for granted gifts and assets that are too close to us, so common to our everyday life that we don't even notice them anymore.

- What are some gifts or assets that you might take for granted?
- What are gifts that allow you to survive?
- What are gifts that allow our congregation to survive?
- What are some assets you dislike but rely on anyway?

We also overlook assets that are uncommon, or that we don't use every day.

- What are some assets that you might overlook, because they are "out of sight, out of mind?"
- What did you used to be good at?
- What are some assets that you only use on special occasions?
- What are some far-away assets?
- What are some invisible assets?
- What are some assets that no one seems to notice but you?
- What's a special place you know about?
- What's a surprising group of people around here?
- What are we all really good at together, but don't recognize it?

3. **Think bigger.**

Often, we don't think of our assets in one context because we think they go with another context. These are often valuable assets to recognize because they point us to a bigger picture when we are Connecting the Dots.

- What are some assets that don't go here?
- What are some contacts or resources you can access in your work life?
- What are some skills you use in your family life?
- What are some ideas and methods you use in public life and politics?
- What kinds of culture or recreation do you enjoy?

- What's the craziest thing you do?
- What's the most unusual group in the community?

Third-glance Questions. These deeper questions help demonstrate and use the asset-mapping concepts of abundance, relationship, and open-sum action. They lay the foundation for the next two steps in the process. These questions make wonderful tools for groups that might be stuck. For instance, if someone brings up questions about needs, I'll "turn the inside out" with the needs transformation exercise, described later in this chapter.

These third-glance questions can even be used as short stand-alone exercises. You could try one with a group separate from the Quick and Simple Experience, or as a follow-up to the Quick and Simple Experience to address a particular situation. For example, the six degrees of connection process, described later in this chapter, works well with leadership development and recruitment. Asset-based appreciation, also described later in this chapter, is a good way to start a planning process from an asset-based approach.

But don't use more than one of these deeper questions in the course of a Quick and Simple Experience. One will be plenty to chew on.

These questions can be used on their own as short exercises to demonstrate the asset-mapping concepts of abundance, relationship building, and open-sum action.

---

1. **Turn the inside out.**

    Sometimes participants are highly focused on needs instead of assets. They may feel strongly that those needs are important—and undoubtedly they are. As a facilitator, you can use that strong emotion. Because inside every need is an asset. This simple truth can be revealed by asking questions like:
    - What are assets that have become clear from crisis?
    - What are needs you can use as assets? (Consider the old saying, "When you are handed lemons, make lemonade.")

> Third-glance Questions
> 1. Turn the inside out.
> 2. Widen the circle.
> 3. Look back.

Try This: Needs Transformation Exercise

This tool can help participants turn needs inside out, in order to recognize assets. It's based on the simple idea that needs point to things we care about. When we say we need something, we are trying to strengthen or protect something that we care about, which is an asset.

We turn a need inside out when we identify the thing we care about. Saying that we have a need points us to something we already have and value. The asset is not the thing we lack; the asset is the thing we want to strengthen and protect.

- Ask participants to name needs for their congregation.
- Choose one need. What's the asset inside that need? In other words, what's the thing they care about, the thing that this need points to?
- Select another need and do it again, until participants see that this works for every need.

Inside every need is an asset.

CONSULTANT'S JOURNAL

Inside every need is an asset.

In one congregation, people identified "not enough people sitting in the pews" as a need. Then they turned this need inside out. They considered what they cared about that this need pointed to. One person named "the people who do come to worship" as an asset. Another said, "our community of faith." A third called out, "the joy in God that we want to share and witness."

In another congregation, people listed "lack of drug rehabilitation services" as a need. One person named, "the rehab services that we do have." Another said, "the talents and potential of drug-addicted people, that we want to uplift and employ." A third said, "our opportunity to walk with others in mission."

It's sometimes difficult at first, to turn needs inside out. But after a while the assets become crystal clear. Then we realize that there is no need that can't be transformed this way. Truly, inside every need is an asset.

2. **Widen the circle.**

   Sometime during the Quick and Simple Experience, someone may ask, "Assets of what? Assets of our congregation, our family, our community, or ourselves?" The answer to that question is "Yes!" Our personal gifts are assets to our family. Our congregational strengths are gifts to our family. An asset is an asset. The idea is to widen our circle of vision and engagement.

These questions simply ask the participants to recognize assets by widening their field of vision.

- What are some of your personal assets?
- What are some of your family assets?
- What are some of your congregation's assets?
- What are some assets of the community around your church or temple?
- What are some assets of your larger faith community?

Try This: Six Degrees of Connection

Here's a more powerful way to widen our circle of engagement with other people.

Choose someone famous or powerful. Think of how you might reach that person. Think of someone you know, who knows someone, who might know someone who could contact that person.

Think of how you might use these kinds of connections to get things done. Who do you know who just might be an asset to the work of the congregation? Who owes you a favor? Who has an interest that overlaps with one or more of your interests?

---

3. **Look back.**

The usefulness of discovering all these assets will become clearer in the next step, Connecting the Dots. But if you run across doubters, remember that we use our assets all the time. Looking back, we can see this is true, and recognize some key assets in the process.

You can help participants recognize that we always build on assets by asking questions like:

- What are some of our cultural assets?
- What are some of our historical assets?

STEERING CLEAR OF DEAD ENDS

Recognizing Our Assets is an open-ended process in which the participants generate a list. The list is not meant to be complete in any way. It's just some of the assets that this group of people thought of at this time in this place. The same group could come together tomorrow and generate a different list. A different group would identify different things. That's part of the point: We each see different gifts.

In group work and organizational planning, we are used to a decision-making process that closes down options. This often happens when people generate lists. A group might do a needs assessment to decide which services to provide. Or they might list the critical priorities for their group, to eliminate some of the possibilities. The closing down of options may be perfectly appropriate but it comes as a cost. If your interest isn't on the list, you're out of luck. "You should have been at the meeting," is the often-heard response.

Try This: Asset-Based Appreciation Exercise

This process illustrates how congregations and communities already use asset mapping without knowing it or calling it that. This is also a process that you can use either within or separate from the Quick and Simple Asset-Mapping Experience.

Ask participants to name victories and successes that have happened in and around the congregation.

Choose one of those successes. Ask participants the following two questions:

- What individual and congregational assets were connected to make that success possible?
- What does that tell you?

If participants approach this part of the Quick and Simple Asset-Mapping Process as a closing-down process, they could be beginning on the wrong track. They could worry that they do not have all the assets on the table. They could worry that they are not getting to name their fair share of assets, or that people who aren't present don't have a voice in the determination of the list.

The easiest way to avoid this dead end is to tell people, "We're just brainstorming a list." This is simply some of our assets—we'd never be able to catalog them all. We are having fun with an experience that is meaningful and positive for our community, but we are not making decisions for other people."

Remind people that they are not narrowing their choices; they are widening them. They certainly will want to widen the circle to people who are not present. That's the whole point of asset mapping, to create a snowball of faith and action. From one Quick and Simple Experience, we can each go out and facilitate other Asset-Mapping Experiences. To the list we generate, we can add the results of other groups in and around the congregation. The more assets we recognize the better.

Keys for Recognizing Our Assets

Keep It Simple

As you can see from the list of sample asset questions, congregations and organizations have numerous assets, and there are many ways to see them. In the Quick and Simple Experience, stick with just a few approaches. Ask no more than 10 of these questions and save the others for another time. Participants will generate more than enough assets to work with.

Take Advantage of Community

The key advantage to this process over the Personal Asset Starter is the group dynamic. Participants will get ideas from each other. One person's blind spot is another person's insight. Encourage participants to talk out loud during this process. The energy will be infectious.

Turn Needs into Assets

At first, some participants may name *needs* instead of *assets*, just because that's what we are used to doing. Giving a few gentle reminders usually works early on. But in some circumstances, some groups work harder than others on the half-full cup perspective. Some or all of the participants are highly focused on needs and deficits. When that happens, don't simply insist on sticking to asset language. Don't run away from it either. Face it head on, by using the needs transformation exercise described above.

Encourage Specificity

The more specific the assets that participants recognize, the more meaningful this process will be. Specific assets are also more useful for Connecting the Dots. Encourage specificity by giving an example, as described under The Process, above.

The Main Thing to Remember

When participants go through several rounds of asset identification, they will recognize layer after layer of assets that they had previously overlooked. Taken together, the result of all the participants' thinking will amaze even the most jaded of participants. Ask people what they think, and someone is sure to say, "Wow, look at all the assets we have!" And they will be right!

Chapter 6

Step Two

Connecting the Dots

WHAT HAPPENS

> **AFFINITY**
> We uncover the value of our gifts by connecting them to the gifts of other people. We brainstorm new actions that become possible by linking existing assets. We discover ways to act on our faith.

The half-full cup is only the beginning. Something amazing happens when we focus on assets—we realize that we can put our gifts together to create something new.

In Connecting the Dots, we draw connections between assets. The connections are not abstract categorizations. We do not identify similarities or differences. We brainstorm real *actions*, the things that we can do by putting existing assets together in new ways.

Connecting the Dots creates a bridge between what is and what can be. From one viewpoint, Connecting the Dots is an act of imagination that comes with its own building blocks and concludes with practical results. From another viewpoint, the process is solid planning that remains hopeful and open ended.

Connecting the Dots works best as a group process, because the different perspectives of group participants complement each other. We each see assets in different ways, and we each find different ways connect assets. Together, we spark our collective imagination.

Participants may be amazed and proud of what they come up with. Also, participants will have affirmed the value of each other's gifts by using them in concrete ways to get things done.

THE FACILITATOR'S TASK

Groups enjoy this step, and the participants do most of the work! To facilitate Connecting the Dots, you will give the directions to the groups and help them to steer clear of dead-end paths, as we'll discuss in this section.

Groups experience a learning curve with Connecting the Dots. At first, groups may be quiet. The participants might feel confused. Then, someone suggests a connection between two assets. Another participant sees an asset that fits, too. Soon the group has discovered a cluster of assets, and the process has taken off.

Facilitation in this part is being an active witness to this group process. What I mean by *active witness* is that you will support the groups' progress without participating yourself. You will float between groups, watch participants working together, encourage ideas, and answer questions. Sometimes a facilitator will help a group find that spark that really gets the process going.

Be an active witness to the group process.

But the real genius of the process lies in the group dynamic. Participants will use their personal skills and styles to get things done in unique and fascinating ways. As facilitator, you will end up watching in wonder. The hardest part of the process will be telling people to stop!

THE PROCESS

First, describe the idea of Connecting the Dots to participants. Then, direct participants to tape their asset sheets on the wall. Ask participants to brainstorm ways to connect the dots. Visit with groups to make sure that they are on track.

Describing the Idea

Tell participants that they will make things happen by creating a new link between two or more existing assets. Together, participants will create new links by moving around the sheets of assets.

Give one or more examples of connecting the dots, such as:
- "When we put our Bibles together with our faith and the fellowship room, we have Bible study."

- "If we put my broken car together with Brian's mechanical skills and the youth group, we'd have a car repair clinic."
- "If we put the Sunday school classrooms together with Mrs. Coleman's friends who take in kids on weekdays, we'd have a day care center."

CONSULTANT'S JOURNAL

I wonder about the meaning of development.

I had been a developer for 20 years when asset-thinking pioneer John McKnight said to me, "Development is creating a link between two or more existing assets." Before that, I never could have explained the idea so simply. Since then, I cannot explain it any other way.

I began to wonder if this definition worked for every kind of development. I discovered that the definition helps describe concepts ranging from congregational development to community development; from urban development to rural development; from organizational development to economic development. I found that it also helps explain other kinds of development, like personal and family development, stewardship and mission development.

In each case, we make things happen by putting assets together, by sharing our gifts. Something new emerges from the mix. We get a whole that is greater than the sum of the parts. Where does the extra bit come from? What can explain this but grace? I began to think that maybe all kinds of development are faith development.

Try This: The Barn-Raising Example

In the pioneer days, when farmers wanted to build a place to house the livestock, they couldn't call up contractors and ask for bids or apply for a grant. What did they do? They had a barn raising.

Ask participants to name some of the assets that were connected to make a barn raising. They'll say things like:

- Wood
- Carpentry skills
- Labor
- Design
- Food
- Neighbors, family, and friends
- Land
- Farm (the economic asset that the barn is used for)

When we connect these assets, we make something new happen—a barn raising. An *action*. And from that action, the farmer got a new asset—a barn. Plus, other gifts emerged from the event: the neighbors learned new skills, built relationships, and created a larger sense of community.

> You might end by observing that things are not so different today: "What do we call something like that now? Habitat for Humanity? A mission church?"

Choosing the Focus

You can ask participants to connect the dots, and they will come up with ideas that make sense to them. You do not have to provide any more direction than that. Often, the goals and directions of the group arise from this type of exercise. It becomes a kind of backward visioning process—we read our vision from the actions we take together. For example, if after participants brainstorm, they indicate interest in several musical ministries, then the congregation might focus its stewardship and evangelism around music. We sometimes call this *visionary* asset mapping.

You can tailor the process of Connecting the Dots for a particular purpose. Say, "Connect the Dots to do _____."

In this stage, you can tailor the process to fit your situation. By making a very small change, you can target asset mapping to accomplish a particular mission or to organize a particular project. We call this *targeted* asset mapping. You can do this by filling in the blank when you direct the group and say: "Connect the Dots to do _____."

Here are some examples of targeted asset mapping:

- **Target: To do God's will**
  If the group did the Optional Jumping-Off Point at the beginning, then participants have thought about the question, "What is God's will for this community?" For this part, participants would connect the dots to accomplish God's will for their community. In fact, that might be the best direction for the group, even if they did not talk about God's will at the beginning.

- **Target: To accomplish a group mission**
  You can tailor the effort to the overall purpose of the group. If the group is the stewardship committee, for example, you might suggest that participants connect the dots to strengthen stewardship in their congregation. If the group is a church governing board, you could give a direction such as, "Connect the Dots to strengthen your congregation in mission."

- **Target: To address a specific situation**

  Participants may express concern about a particular situation. Perhaps, they are kicking off a campaign or are feeling stuck on a project. Maybe there has been some kind of crisis in the community or the church. The participants could focus on that situation. You might say, "Connect the dots to strengthen your faith and follow God's call in this situation."

Whether you choose to do visionary or target asset mapping, Connecting the Dots will open up possibilities for the group and its ministry. The finish will be broader than the start. Participants will make new connections and see a bigger picture.

What would happen if you connected two
or more of the assets on the wall?

The results of connecting the dots to strengthen stewardship, for example, might include one-on-one visits and small group meetings that touch on questions of faith. You might easily consider these evangelism actions. Asset mapping that targets evangelism could lift up plans to invite the wider community to use a church's buildings, which might also look like a social-justice initiative. Overlaps like these are not a mistake. They indicate the wonderful power of asset mapping.

Giving Directions

As facilitator, you will tell participants to work in groups, in order to connect their assets. Below are specific directions that you can give to participants. The group process can be noisy and busy, so it is helpful to review these directions with participants before they begin.

1. Participants will work with the same groups in which they created their asset sheets. Each group will use a section of the wall. Ask groups to find a space on the wall that is big enough for everyone to gather, work, and see together.
2. Participants will tape asset sheets on the wall in their area. It does not matter what order the assets are in, or who wrote which one for which question. The sheets simply need to be visible.
3. Everyone in the group will gather by the wall that holds their group's assets. Tell participants to take time to look at the assets. Ask participants, "What would happen if you connected two or more of the assets on the wall?"

4. Tell participants that when they see a possible connection, they should move the connecting assets to a new place. Put them together so that it is clear that they are being linked. As participants talk about it, they will see more connections and the cluster will grow. Participants will end up connecting the dots for several clusters of assets.

5. Explain to participants that when a cluster of assets takes a certain shape, they will give the action a title or name that will describe the action, so that other people can understand it. Write the title down on another sheet of paper and tape it by the cluster to identify the action. Often, having the title helps participants think of other connections.

Active Witnessing

The groups will work on their own. As the facilitator, you are not participating. You will float from group to group, listen in, and offer friendly suggestions where appropriate. You can be an active witness.

Remember, groups usually start slowly, and then gather steam. If the group is quiet, they might be thinking. You can encourage a group by saying, "What assets could we put together to get something done? Choose a couple of assets to get started."

Participants will end up with several clusters of assets, each representing a possible action and each with its own title.

If a group is feeling stuck and really cannot get started, you can spark their thinking by moving two or three assets together and saying, "What if we connected these assets? What could we get done with that?" When someone suggests a possible action, affirm him or her. Encourage participants to think of some other assets that would go with that action.

Try This: The Weirdest Assets

Connecting the Dots is an act of imagination. Often, it is the weirdest assets that help us to think outside the box. You can use these assets to help any group get unstuck.

Ask participants, "What are the two weirdest assets up on the wall?" Or instruct, "Choose two assets that you do not think go together at all."

Ask participants to think of an action that would put those two assets together in a new way.

If a group is spending all of its time linking assets to a single action, suggest that they start working on a couple more clusters. If a group is making many new clusters with only a few assets in each, encourage them to select a few clusters to consider more fully. Groups should end up with several action options, perhaps two to six.

> **CONSULTANT'S JOURNAL**
> ### *Naming can be fun.*
> *People enjoy making up interesting titles or names for the actions they brainstorm. I have been fascinated by the way this energy and creativity seems to come from the enthusiasm the group has over their work. The enthusiasm feeds on itself. When someone comes up with a great name for a cluster of assets, other participants are motivated to think of new connections.*
>
> *Here are some examples of names that I have seen groups create and use:*
> - *Fairways to Heaven: Connecting one person's love for golf with a youth center at the church to create a golfing event to raise money for church youth development.*
> - *Motivating Male Ministry: Connecting the table of men who have coffee together with members' deep spirituality and financial savvy to spark constructive ministries.*
> - *Paper Puzzle: Connecting puzzle-solving skills with three different types of hymnals, office equipment and supplies, and the commitment to welcome people to worship to find an accessible yet paper-friendly way to present the liturgy.*
> - *God's Green Acres of Joy: Connecting a grassy wooded area with music ministries to stage an outdoor mission festival and worship service.*
> - *Waterfront Worship Festival: Connecting the relationships between local congregations with municipal investment in a waterfront district to create a highly visible and welcoming festival of faith.*

The actions participants brainstorm often highlight networking, showcasing, or bringing together assets and people. In other words, by Connecting the Dots people generate ideas that will further Connect the Dots in action. They think of things like:

- Shared meal
- Talent show
- Clearinghouse for good ideas
- Newsletters and communication
- Peer-to-peer school or classes
- Church or temple community center
- Skill exchanges

- Asset bartering
- Partnerships
- Coalitions
- Job banks
- Sharing faith in worship and prayer

STEERING CLEAR OF DEAD ENDS

Remember, Connecting the Dots is about opening up possibilities not closing them down. Anything that can lead the group to screen out or reduce possibilities is a dead end. That fixed-sum kind of thinking works counter to the asset mapping method and can lead to groups becoming stuck again. As the facilitator, you can watch out for a couple of dead ends and help participants steer clear of them.

No Bad Ideas

Many people are familiar with the idea of group brainstorming and understand the ground rule: there are no bad ideas. Sometimes the craziest thoughts fuel the greatest level of group imagination. Remind group members not to evaluate participants' ideas. Instead, participants are encouraged to support each other, build on each other's ideas, and look for new connections.

> **What groups might come up with**
> Participants will brainstorm actions that combine existing assets in new ways. The specific actions will depend on the assets you identify and the dynamics of the groups involved. The types of actions groups might brainstorm include things like:
> - Projects
> - Events
> - Performances
> - Campaigns
> - Demonstrations
> - Models or pilot projects
> - Celebrations
> - Protests
> - Making things
> - Growing things
> - Fixing things
> - Learning things

Don't Categorize, Connect

It is natural for participants to want to categorize the assets on the wall, to sort assets into groups according to similarities. This is something we have all been taught to do even as even as children. Sorting is often used in various planning methods, even in exercises using a similar sticky-notes approach.

As a facilitator, you can expect someone to do this. Even when you specifically instruct participants to connect assets for action, someone will immediately start to sort the assets on the wall. Someone will suggest that the group begin by getting rid of the duplicates or by stacking them together as one. Someone will start to cluster all the financial assets, youth assets, or natural assets. Don't, Don't, Don't!

You cannot make a snowball with a screen.

When we sort and categorize, we narrow down the choices. We group things together to simplify a complex picture. It is something that is usually part of a process of screening, controlling, or gatekeeping.

When a group begins by sorting or categorizing assets, they get stuck. They end up staring at the nicely sorted categories of assets on the wall and saying, "Now what?" They are not opening up possibilities. They are closing down possibilities. Then they wonder why they cannot think of any new actions!

Now, it's possible that for some people the act of sorting might serve as spark to open creative thinking. I appreciate the analytical mind and I can see how that might work in theory. But, in practice, categorizing is poison to the open-sum process of Connecting the Dots. It is like adding criticism to the process of brainstorming—it cuts against the grain of the approach and derails the group dynamic. Or as I tell people, "You cannot make a snowball with a screen." All you get is powder.

> **Try This: Avoid the Dreaded Categorizing**
> What can a facilitator do to help participants steer clear of categorizing?
> 1. Include a caution against categorizing in your initial directions, using examples like the barn raising to show what you mean by connecting the dots for action instead of categorizing the assets.
> 2. When you are witnessing groups in action, watch for categorizing early on. If you see it, remind people of the directions and examples. Give them another example. I tell people, "If we put all the trees and lumber assets in the Wood category, all we would have is a big pile of wood. It's only when the wood is connected with carpentry skills and land and food and such that we have a barn raising."

KEYS FOR CONNECTING THE DOTS

Keep It Simple

Connecting the Dots is harder to describe than do. Almost every small group of participants will understand the idea with very little direction. Do not make it seem more complicated than it is. When in doubt, get into the process as quickly as possible. Use your own style, follow your own instincts, and call on the ideas and approaches in this section to increase your comfort with facilitation.

Open It Up

Remind participants that there are no bad ideas. We are brainstorming connections, not putting assets into categories. Encourage participants to build on their weirdest assets to get rolling.

Connecting the Dots demonstrates what we all know how to do: building relationships.

Stay Out of the Way

The creativity happens in the group. Witness the group process and encourage participants. Only step in if you see the group heading toward a dead end.

THE MAIN THING TO REMEMBER

Connecting the Dots opens us to the possibilities inherent in the gifts we have received. We break out of our old ways of thinking by remembering and using what is valuable about our existing assets and our history. When we combine the familiar and the new, we guide our imaginations onto practical but open paths. The result is useful innovation and faithful creativity.

Set it up, step back, and watch it unfold. Unexpected things will happen. We get unstuck. We renew ourselves. People will laugh and work together in unexpected ways.

Though the process may be new and the results unexpected, participants will find themselves drawing on familiar experience and skill. Connecting the Dots demonstrates something we all know how to do: building relationships. When we are Connecting the Dots, we are finding affinity between other people's interests and our own. We change "them" into "part of us."

Chapter 7

Step Three

Voting with Our Feet

> **RELEASE**
> We give each other permission to follow our hearts and to do what is right for us, which leads us to a whole that is greater than the sum of the parts. We become part of something bigger.

*From the group reports, invite people to choose
the action that they most want to participate
in and stand next to it.
That is all there is to it.*

Voting with Our Feet is the payoff of congregational asset mapping.

This step is the quickest and simplest part of the Quick and Simple Congregational Asset-Mapping Experience. As a facilitator, you will ask the groups of participants to report on the actions they have generated. You will invite people to choose the action in which they most want to participate and to stand next to it. That is all there is to it.

And yet, for many people, Voting with Our Feet is the most meaningful and powerful part of the process. That's because it's different from the kind of process we have come to expect—where we are required to narrow down choices and agree to a master plan, even if it excludes some of our assets and interests. In Voting with Our Feet, we find our calling in the union of our gifts and the affinities we discover with one another. We give each other permission to follow our hearts.

In this process, we live out our faith that the right things will happen when we follow our hearts. First, our hearts and our faith will lead each of us to do what we believe is right. Second, we will put God's gifts together and we will find the affinities that make it possible for us to get things done. Finally, when our faithful efforts are taken together, they will add up to a whole that is bigger than all of us.

We cannot control the outcome of Voting with Our Feet. It is a leap of faith. We place ourselves in God's hands, and that is enough.

> **CONSULTANT'S JOURNAL**
> ### We make the path by walking it.
> The leaders of one congregation told me they were "good at planning, but not at implementation." The pastor and the council would work well together at setting goals and choosing projects to accomplish those goals. But the projects always seemed to fall flat because few people volunteered to lead.
>
> A funny thing happened after asset mapping. Three people found out that they shared an interest in the Internet and worked together to develop and maintain a church Web site. Two people picked up their old brass instruments to play for worship services. Two new golf foursomes were created.
>
> From there, the energy in the congregation snowballed. More members took up Sunday school teaching, the building campaign picked up new leadership, and one member from the congregation was elected to the regional board. In addition, to everyone's astonishment, eight people stood up to run for three open seats on the church council!
>
> When I asked the leaders why they thought this had happened, they did not say, "We followed a new system of congregational leadership development." They said it was because the members of the congregation had learned more about each other. They stopped planning projects that people did not want to do and started giving each other permission to do what stirred their passions. In short, they voted with their feet.

The Facilitator's Task

Your job as the facilitator now is to be the *cheerleader*. You are essentially helping participants widen their circles of mutual trust and faith, from their small groups to the larger gathering.

Affirm the good brainstorming that people have done in groups. Help participants see themselves as part of an exciting community that has a lot of potential. Clap for the group reports. Point out the good things you see in people's ideas. Celebrate the relationships that participants have created with each other in their groups. Encourage participants to listen to each other in the larger gathering.

Invite participants to show their faith in each other by following their hearts and finding their calling in the larger agenda. If people have a hard time choosing between options, tell them something like, "That's a good thing! Choose something and see what happens." What does happen will inspire you all.

THE PROCESS

First, we share our ideas with each other. Then we follow our hearts. Participants remain standing during Voting with Our Feet, to physically engage in the process.

Try This: Why Listen?
Participants may think that they already know what happens with the report, based on similar group processes that they have been involved with. Often, participants think that it is boring to listen to the reports of other groups.

But this is no ordinary report. In Voting with Our Feet, we're building on the connections and trust that participants developed in the small groups and broadening these to the whole gathering.

You can highlight the community-building aspect of Voting with Our Feet by poking gentle fun at our negative assumptions about reporting processes. Ask participants, "What are we supposed to do during group reports?" Smile and answer the question yourself: "Go to sleep until it's your turn to vote, right?" Hopefully you will have surprised them.

Explain that this is one time when participants have to listen to each other's reports, because this is Voting with Our Feet. After the reports, each participant will go and stand next to the action they most want to participate in. Tell participants, "You have to know what you are voting for. You have to listen because you have to act."

Reporting

Tell the participants that the groups will present the actions they developed to the whole gathering. Go around the room, from group to group, pointing to the clusters on the wall. Ask each group of participants to describe what they have put together. Invite all participants to move around the room with you, so that they can hear the reports and see the asset clusters on the wall.

You can depend on spokespersons to emerge from each group. Sometimes one person reports on all the actions; other times different individuals report on different projects. Ask, "Who will report on this?" and be patient.

Ask the spokesperson to name the particular action and then to talk briefly about the assets the group connected to arrive at the idea. Repeat the names of the actions, praise the group, and lead the gathering in clapping for the group's work.

Voting with Our Feet

Invite participants to stand next to the action that God is calling them to. Allow time for the participants to review the options before them. When the time allotted is running low, invite stragglers to make a decision.

Creating an Instant Work Plan

Ask participants to look around the room. Make sure it is clear who has voted for what. If necessary, ask people which particular action they are standing by.

You can tell participants that they have created an instant work plan. When participants look around the room, they will see concrete actions, the gifts that will make those actions possible, some of the connections necessary to get things done, and people who care enough about the actions to work on them.

---

*By Recognizing Our Assets, Connecting the Dots,
and Voting with Our Feet, we have created
an instant work plan.*

The instant work plan is not the only outcome that is visible from Voting with Our Feet. Ask participants, "Looking around the room at all of this, what do you notice?" Allow time for people to think and offer comments. This may be a good time to transition into the reflection step by asking questions such as:

- Did anything surprise you? What connections or actions might have opened up your thinking?
- Are there any actions that nobody's standing next to? What, if anything should we do about that?
- What about if only one person is standing next to an action? What, if anything, should we say to them?
- What connections do you see between the actions brainstormed by different groups?
- Taken together, what would these actions accomplish?

Steering Clear of Dead Ends

We are more familiar with voting with our hands than voting with our feet. As part of a group, we are typically presented with a choice for group decision, and we raise our hands to signal our individual preferences. The whole group is supposed to abide by the winning decision.

Voting with our feet is different. Instead of all of us deciding what every one of us will do, we give each other permission to decide for ourselves. We do not control or coerce. The group action comes from the self-determined actions of the individual participants.

People get this right away, and they are glad to have the permission to do what they want to do. Some may have difficulty choosing between two or more actions. I have seen people lie on the floor in order to "stand" across two or more actions!

In the voluntary world of congregations and communities, we always vote with our feet. Voting with our feet is both the action and the lesson.

Is this vote for real? Some people may have questions about a particular action they are voting for and wonder if they are really committing to something. Of course, commitment comes with action. If a participant thinks an idea is great, he or she will work on it. If a participant thinks it is a nice idea but is not ready to act, he or she will do nothing. Isn't that the way it always goes? In the voluntary world of congregations and communities, we always vote with our feet. We choose to do the things we do.

Participants will vote with their feet one way or another, and people recognize this. Voting with our feet is both the action and the lesson. A dead end is impossible.

Keys for Voting with Our Feet

Keep It Simple

Keep the reports moving along, politely and positively. Give people the direction to stand by the action they would most like to participate in, and step out of the way.

73

Affirm and Celebrate the Groups

Repeat what you hear from the groups and show appreciation for their work. Group members discovered and showed affinity for each other as they Connected the Dots. When you applaud and commend the groups after their reports, you invite participants to extend that affinity to everyone in the gathering. You help to widen the circle.

There Are No Right Answers

Do not worry about how the vote will turn out. Participants will vote from their hearts. That is the point!

Look Around

Ask participants to look around and notice what they see. The lessons of this part are physical and visual. How do you feel about being part of this group? What does that tell you about yourself, your congregation, and your community of faith?

The Main Thing to Remember

Taken together, our actions are something extraordinary.

We could argue that one action or another action is more significant. We might fear that if we do not control what happens, important things will not get done. We might fear that we will not do what is right.

We take a leap of faith when we give each other permission to follow God's call. We release control to God. We trust that God's call to each one of us will benefit the whole.

Taken together, our actions become something extraordinary. Your gain is my gain is our gain.

The actions that some of us work on strengthen the actions of others. Your Bible study supports their stewardship project, which enhances the congregation's evangelism efforts, which increase the effectiveness of several ministries, and comes back to strengthen worship and prayer and so on. We each contribute to each other's interest because we all benefit from the collective effort. Your gain is my gain is our gain.

Our community of faith is a whole that is bigger than the sum of its parts.

Chapter 8

Reflecting on Asset Mapping

An End, a Beginning, a Renewal

What Happens

> **REFLECTION**
> We learn from what we've done and we do it some more! We reflect on what we have experienced, which compels us to use what we know. We feel a building momentum.

After Voting with Our Feet, the asset-mapping process is over. Or is it? In traditional planning, we think first about why we should act, then we figure out how to act, and finally we act. The asset mapping process moves backwards. When we collect and connect our assets, we are acting on thankfulness and faith. Then we figure out *why* that works for us the way it does. The last part of the Quick and Simple Congregational Asset-Mapping Experience, reflecting on the process, is also the beginning. We bear witness to where our faith has led us. We ask ourselves what we experienced and why we experienced it. We learn from doing, and that further strengthens our faith. And so we are compelled to act on our faith.

Right now, at the end of the Quick and Simple Congregational Asset-Mapping Experience, give the group a chance to reflect and talk with each other, even if only for a few minutes. The purpose of this group discussion is to capture the immediacy of the moment, before feelings fade and impressions are lost. There is too much energy in the room to let the moment pass!

Recognize that reflection may start at this time, with this group of people, in this room, but it will not end here. Reflection will continue in the clean-up time, on the ride home, at work tomorrow, and at the next committee meeting. Reflection will continue as participants share their gifts with people who were not even involved in the session. Some of the best learning from the experience will not come until participants are involved in another experience, see a connection, and put that learning into action again.

In the larger view, this is neither an end
nor a beginning, but a renewal
of faith and witness.

CONSULTANT'S JOURNAL
Sometimes talking is all it takes.
A lay leader from a rural community shared with me a moment of reflection that happened months after her congregation had done asset mapping together.

"Our evangelism and outreach committee was having a meeting about whether we should keep doing these Gifts and Talents surveys that don't get used. A few of us on the committee were talking while we were waiting for the meeting to get started. We discovered that all of us were bowlers. We thought, why not form a church bowling team? Then we talked about other people outside of our congregation, who we knew were bowlers, and someone said, 'Why not see if they wanted to be on the team?'

"I started thinking about bowling as an evangelism strategy, and I just cracked up laughing. This is something that could actually reach some of the bowlers I know, and draw them into church and a stronger faith life. Finally, it hit me that this is like the asset-mapping thing we did. That is what Connecting the Dots and Voting with Our Feet were all about. I realized that instead of a survey, we could be talking to each other about our gifts and talents. We could find new ways share them. We might be surprised at the paths to faith and witness we discover."

We've started, restarted, or simply fueled a cycle of action and reflection that will stick with us as long as we choose. In the larger view, this is neither an end nor a beginning, but a renewal of faith and witness.

It's exciting! We are part of a movement. We are building momentum. We are creating a snowball of faith and witness.

The Facilitator's Task

Voices will buzz throughout the room. Participants will want to talk about what they learned. They will have interesting things to say to each other. The facilitator's task is to open up this discussion.

Part of this task is simply procedural. Your job is to chair the meeting. You will invite participants to reflect together on the process of asset mapping. Call on the individuals who wish to speak and make sure that everyone who wants to speak gets a turn.

Part of your task is also conceptual. You will open up the discussion to extraordinary concepts and lessons. There is something intuitive about this affirming, connecting, open experience. You can get at these lessons by asking questions that probe participant's feelings. You can encourage participants to draw connections—between the steps, between each other, or between their faith and this experience.

Facilitate reflection by opening up the discussion, both in process and in concept.

You can also share the open-sum idea: *your gain is my gain is our gain.* Ask participants to reflect on how this idea springs from asset mapping and what it has to do with our faith.

THE PROCESS

Ask participants a variety of questions about the asset-mapping experience, including questions about participant's feelings during the process, the tangible results, the open-sum idea, and using and sharing asset mapping with others.

Here are sample discussion questions to help you to guide the discussion. Choose questions based on the time you have available and the interests of your group. If you wish, you can write the responses on a flip chart.

Gathering Initial Impressions

Catch participant's impressions while they are standing by the actions they voted for. This captures the feeling of being in community together. You might ask:

- What do you notice around the room?

Sensing the Power of Faith in Community

Ask participants to talk about their emotional response to asset mapping. This will help them to see the value of the asset-mapping experience. Try these questions:

77

- How did it feel to think about your assets?
- How did it feel to put your assets on the wall together with the assets of your group?
- How did you feel when you were Connecting the Dots? (Often, at least some participants will say it was confusing at first, and suddenly came together.)
- How did you feel when you Voted with Your Feet?

Recognizing Results

Results are an important motivator to people. Give participants an opportunity to talk about both the expected and the unexpected results.

- What surprised you in the experience? Why?
- When you connected the dots, what kinds of actions emerged?
- What about the actions you arrived at? Are they possible? Could you do any or all of these things? What would happen if you did?
- What have you accomplished already?

Your gain is my gain is our gain. *How does this open-sum idea spring from asset mapping? What does this have to do with our faith?*

Thinking about Open-Sum Dynamics

Ask participants about the open-sum nature of what they just did. Remember, a process is open-sum if it follows the pattern: *your gain is my gain is our gain.* See if that dynamic underlies what participants are taking away from the experience. Start by asking about the open-sum idea of Recognizing Assets.

- How much grace is there in the world? If you get more grace, do I get less?
- How much faith is there in the world? If I get more faith, does it come out of your supply? Or does your faith strengthen mine, and my faith increase yours, and our faith grow on others?
- How many assets are there in our community? If we Connect the Dots, do we use up our assets or do we create new assets to use more and more?

Ask about the open-sum idea of Connecting the Dots.

- What happened when we connected the assets?
- What can we accomplish in collaboration that we could not accomplish on our own?

Finally, ask about the open-sum dynamic of Voting with Our Feet.

- What happens when we brainstorm an action and no one votes with their feet to do that action?
- If only two people want to connect their assets to act in faith, should we say no?
- What connections do you see between the actions on the wall?
- If we give each other permission to act on our assets and interests, will we grow apart or grow together? Will we lose to each other or will we all gain?

Using and Sharing Asset Mapping

As the facilitator, use these questions to encourage participants to share the lessons of asset building with others in widening circles of connection and mission.

- Can you apply what you did here to your daily life?
- Is asset building something you think you can use in your work around the congregation?
- Now that you have participated in this process, do you think you could facilitate the Quick and Simple Congregational Asset-Mapping Experience with others? Maybe if you had a partner?

CONSULTANT'S JOURNAL

How do I avoid overselling the amazing?

My faith has been strengthened by the reflections I have heard from participants in the Quick and Simple Congregational Asset-Mapping Experience. When people say, "it's amazing," "it's empowering," and even, "it changed my life," I am truly moved.

But I am suspicious of unbalanced superlatives. When everything is described as positive and great, I wonder if we are getting an honest and critical view. So I make sure that I listen for the downbeat undercurrents. That is when I really feel the Holy Spirit working.

I asked one group, "How did it feel to Connect the Dots?" People said, "confusing," and "overwhelming," and even, "a mess." I made sure to repeat what I heard and write it down on the flip chart for everyone to see.

Then participants went further. "It was confusing at first. Then suddenly things started to fall into place," said one. "That's right. I didn't think we could do anything with that mess of assets on the wall, but we got one idea and then we just couldn't stop."

"Our beginning confusion made our later success all the more amazing," said another. "It's as though the mess created the powerful experience."

> *I am still struggling with how I present asset mapping to others. I worry that the uplifting experience I have had might sound suspicious. I know how it would sound to me. So I try to let people experience it for themselves. And then I witness their faith rising from the mess.*

Steering Clear of Dead Ends

Positive experience cannot be forced. True reflection is open ended. There are no wrong answers, only individual and collective impressions. Those impressions will lead participants to act and grow in faith.

Be sincerely interested in the reflections of participants. Let the participants do the rest.

- As facilitator, you will feel an affinity with the group. Your contribution is to be sincerely interested in the responses of participants. Resist any temptation to dwell on or steer the group discussion toward either positive or negative responses. Ask questions that open up concepts for participants to consider. Offer the open-sum idea as a possible framework for group reflection. Let the participants do the rest.

Keys for Reflecting on Asset Mapping

Keep It Simple

This is not a lecture. This is a starting point for group reflection. With a few simple questions, participant response will be rich.

Open Up Discussion

Chair the discussion in order to give everyone a chance to talk. Choose a variety of the sample questions on feelings and outcomes to give participants a chance to contribute diverse reflections on their experience.

The Main Thing to Remember

We learn by reflecting on experience. The lessons that we draw from asset mapping strengthen our faith and compel us to witness this faith to others.

This motivates us to act again, which leads to more learning—in a positive snowballing cycle of faith and witness.

Group discussion widens the circle and enhances the open-sum effect. Your gain is my gain is our gain. Your reflection makes me think, my reflection makes you think, and together we contribute to a larger group reflection.

Group reflection is itself a model of open-sum dynamics. Your reflection makes me think, my reflection makes you think, and together we contribute to a larger group reflection. Your gain is my gain is our gain.

By facilitating reflection, you are helping the participants to make another turn in a positive cycle. You are helping participants turn their actions into lessons and their lessons into motivation to act.

Open-sum dynamics come alive in the Quick and Simple Congregational Asset-Mapping Experience. The experience demonstrates the lessons. Participants will feel what they learn more than they will think or talk about it. Our true reflection is more action: We celebrate, and do it some more!

PART THREE

The WHY

Why Does Asset Mapping Work?

PEOPLE SMILE AND LAUGH during the Quick and Simple Congregational Asset-Mapping Experience. I have witnessed amazing changes in congregations and communities of faith when they build on their assets. I have been moved by stories of individuals who have tapped the powers of asset mapping and who have witnessed unexpected grace and love. Asset mapping resonates with our faith and strengthens us in community. Why is that?

This last part of the book is about trying to understand why congregational asset mapping works. Chapter 9 explores how asset mapping reinforces positive cycles and open-sum thinking. Chapters 10 and 11 share some lessons of communities of faith and of congregations in particular who have used asset mapping. The epilogue presents lessons drawn from Bible passages that have been read with an assets perspective.

Chapter 9

The Inner Workings of Asset Mapping

Learning from Congregational Asset Mapping

I hear all sorts of personal reactions, comments, and questions at the end of an asset-mapping experience. The most common response is also the simplest: "It's so positive." Participants often express amazement at the energy and ideas that have emerged from the group. Asset mapping profoundly surprises many people. They discover a new tool to tackle old problems.

Others feel less like they have found a new approach and more like they have rediscovered something they've known all along. A person might say, "This is the way I do things all the time. The asset-mapping experience has validated and celebrated what I know."

What is asset mapping to you? Probably, it is both a validation of what you already know and a new tool. If you have volunteered in a congregation, you already knows something about how people work together. Perhaps you have been part of a group that struggled to recruit members, that never seemed to get going, or that drained everybody's energy and time. But, maybe you have also been part of groups that felt energized and enthusiastic, where it was easy and fun to get things done.

Why does one group struggle while another succeeds? Asset mapping gives us new language and a new conceptual framework to address that question. This chapter examines why asset mapping works. While some of this

> **What is asset mapping to you?**
> - A new tool to tackle old problems?
> - Validation of what you have known all along?
> - Both?

assessment may sound new to you, I imagine it may also sound like something you already know.

Modeling Faith in Community

I know that there are many ways to understand the workings of asset mapping, because people have shared many useful and fascinating perspectives with me. From their understanding of psychology, for example, participants tell me that the Quick and Simple Experience takes advantage of a wide variety of human skills and intelligences, including the social, physical, and visual. From his knowledge of brain theory, my colleague Bob Sitze tells me that the Quick and Simple Congregational Asset-Mapping Experience taps into some powerful tendencies of the human brain that lead us to map connections between things. (Sitze's book for the Alban Institute, *Not Trying Too Hard*, is a rich exploration of congregational and faith life from an asset-based perspective.) You will bring your own experience and knowledge to asset mapping. You will grow in your understanding of the process as you share it with others.

I look at asset mapping in light of my experience in communities and congregations. I have been called to work in voluntary, community, and faith-based organizations since I was 12 years old. These experiences have taught me a lot about how people act and interact, and about how we live our lives in communities. I have seen how things tend to stay the same. I have also seen how people work together to make real and lasting change.

Asset mapping models how faith and community work together.

I think of a community as a loosely knit network of people who voluntarily identify with each other. That would include geographic communities like urban neighborhoods and rural communities. It would also include other types of communities, like communities of interest (such as an arts community), or an ethnic community (such as an immigrant Asian-American community). I think of congregations as communities of faith.

I have come to understand that faithfulness is part of every community. Now, faith is a little harder for me to define. When I think of faith, I think of Abraham, who believed in God above all else. In our life and work with other people, faith has a lot to do with trust, hope, love, and even freedom. People who form communities act out of hope and trust. A healthy community empowers its members to express their faith. Faith and community work together.

I think that asset mapping models both faith and community and the connection between the two. When I say *models* I mean that asset mapping demonstrates how faith and community work together by actually engaging us in faithful community practice. When we do the Quick and Simple Experience together, in particular, we are experiencing faith and community in action.

I call the inner workings of this model the open-sum dynamic. The open-sum dynamic is a self-reinforcing cycle—in which positive changes lead to additional positive changes. In communities of faith that use asset mapping, this positive cycle enables them to counter and break out of negative cycles, strengthening both faith and community.

Good Cycles and Bad Cycles

I often think in terms of cycles because I have been struck by the tendency of human behavior to perpetuate itself. Cycles show up everywhere in human life. For example, when a movie is a hit, people may want to see it because it is a hit, so it becomes more of a hit, in a cycle of hype. When a person abuses drugs or alcohol, friends and family may react in ways that the addict only sees as reason for more drug and alcohol abuse. The relationship becomes a cycle of codependency.

These self-perpetuating cycles are central to the work of community developers in particular. When city government and businesses stop reinvesting in an inner-city neighborhood, the area may begin to look run down. In a cycle of disinvestment, residents and investors will not risk investing in development. Something similar happens in rural communities when farm consolidation eliminates jobs and business, leading people to cut back or move out, further reducing local spending and eliminating more jobs and businesses. A suburban mall that was once popular loses customers as the next mall grows and becomes trendy.

I have learned that these human cycles do not just happen by themselves. People make cycles happen. Neither do I think cycles are inevitable. People can change the course of these cycles, and we do, all the time. Families intervene in addiction and break out of codependency. People organize to ignite new community development and reverse disinvestment.

Self-perpetuating cycles start and end with our own mind-set. We think a particular way, so then we act a concurring manner, and then corresponding things happen. But, we can transform our thinking. When we think differently, we act differently. As a result, our life changes.

Building Community from the Inside Out
The pioneers of Asset-Based Community Development are John McKnight and Jody Kretzmann, professors, activists, and friends to

community organizations. I first got to know them in Chicago in the mid-1980s, when I participated in a coalition of grassroots community development organizations. We often asked McKnight and Kretzmann to join us as we gathered to share lessons on how to develop jobs and business in low-income communities. Instead of chasing after companies to locate in our neighborhoods and fill our needs, we decided to take stock of the skills and talents of community residents, and develop businesses around those assets. At that time, around the nation and the world, other community groups were embracing the same idea.

McKnight and Kretzmann noticed a pattern of needs and dependency at work in low-income communities. They observed that social services have often been developed and provided to meet community needs. Hospitals provide services to needy patients, an economic development agency serves needy businesses, or a youth worker serves needy youth. In other words, services have been developed and provided to try to fill client deficiencies.

McKnight and Kretzmann saw that communities did better when they recognized their assets and built on them, instead of depending on outsiders to fill their needs. They encouraged community organizations to look at the half-full cup. They urged service providers, funders, and big institutions to stop focusing on needs and to start focusing on building community capacity. McKnight and Kretzmann's book, *Building Communities from the Inside Out: A Guide to Finding and Mobilizing a Community's Assets*, became the best-selling book in community development history. The asset-based perspective has replaced the needs-based approach even in the mainstream funding and policy-making circles.

Today I realize that what McKnight and Kretzmann were really talking about was replacing a negative cycle with a positive cycle. The negative cycle of needs and dependency (figure 9A) works like this: Service providers organize to meet community needs. For community residents to get access to professional services, they have to describe themselves as needy. The caseworker or the grant officer asks residents what they lack, not what they have. As a result, community members become good at describing their needs and deficiencies. They become needy clients instead of capable citizens. They even compete for services with their neighbors, analyzing in great detail how much needier they are. It becomes a race to the bottom!

The cycle continues as community members overlook their assets and forget about what they can do for themselves. They become increasingly dependent on outside services to fill their needs. Service providers react to fill these needs some more, so needs increase, and on it goes.

Figure 9A: Negative Cycle of Need and Dependency

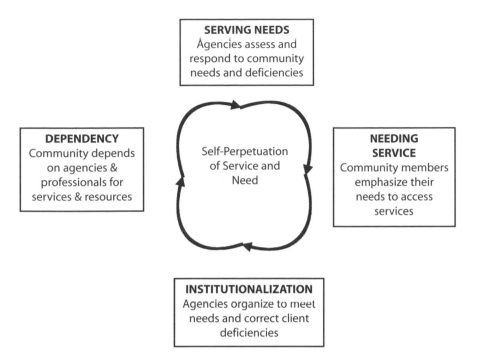

The solution to this negative cycle is to start a positive cycle of assets and opportunity (figure 9B). Community residents start by transforming their perspective. They begin to think of their cup as being half-full rather than half-empty, recognizing their assets instead of their needs. With these assets, they come together to share what they have and get things done. They connect assets by building relationships within their community and discovering common or complementary interests. They use their assets to develop projects, organize events, build businesses, strengthen families, and create social and economic opportunities.

As an active and productive community, then, they are in a good position to leverage outside resources. Instead of going to institutions and service providers as needy clients, community members go as capable citizens. Institutions and service providers recognize that they can get more done by linking their resources to successful community projects. Institutional investment spurs even more development, which creates new assets in the community, and so it continues in a positive cycle of assets and opportunity.

Figure 9B: Positive Cycle of Assets and Opportunity

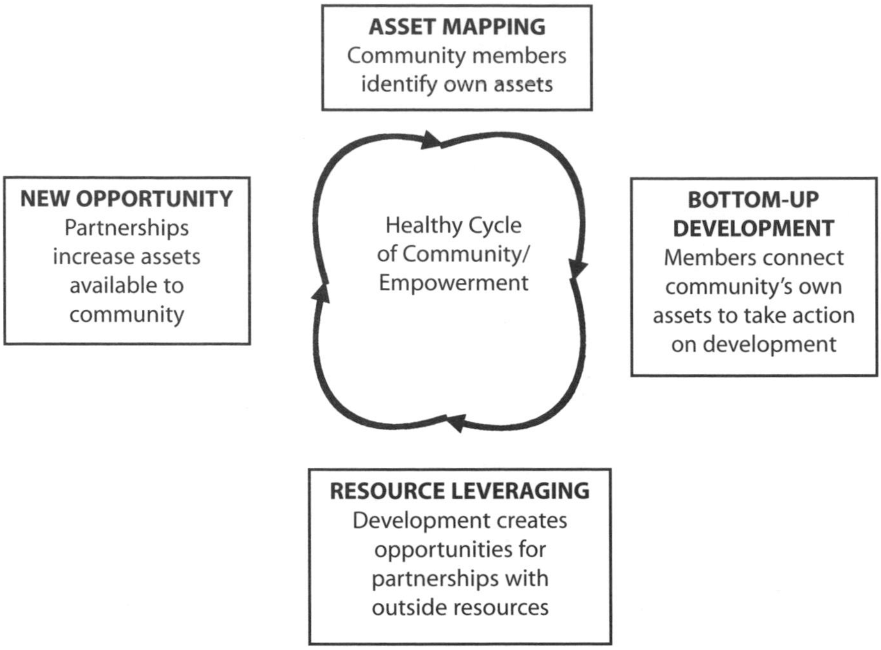

ASSET MAPPING
Community members
identify own assets

NEW OPPORTUNITY
Partnerships
increase assets
available to
community

Healthy Cycle
of Community/
Empowerment

**BOTTOM-UP
DEVELOPMENT**
Members connect
community's own
assets to take action
on development

RESOURCE LEVERAGING
Development creates
opportunities for
partnerships with
outside resources

McKnight and Kretzmann would say they did not invent Asset-Based Community Development. They observed it, lifted it up, and encouraged us all to share it. That is how a positive cycle is strengthened and renewed. Their spirit of openness is what inspired and continues to encourage me to share asset thinking freely and openly, anywhere that I find faithful people who are working together in community.

Negative Cycle of Recruitment

Consider a common cycle in many congregations, a negative cycle of recruitment. Do you ever face problems recruiting volunteers in your congregation? Maybe there is a self-perpetuating cycle at work like this:

Negative Cycle of Recruitment
There is a task in the congregation that people think is difficult or distasteful, so not many people volunteer to serve on that committee, and all of the work falls on a few shoulders. As a result, the task seems more difficult, people drop off the committee, and the work falls on even fewer shoulders, and the cycle continues (see figure 9C).

Figure 9C: Negative Cycle of Recruitment

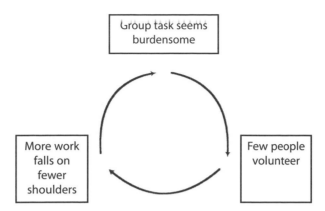

Negative thinking *leads to* negative action, and that negative action *leads to* more negative thinking. Negative cycles may feel like a trap we cannot escape from. The more we despair about the problem, the more negative our thinking becomes, the worse the problem becomes. And here is the difficult part: sometimes the things we think and do about the problem only make things worse. In the negative cycle of recruitment, for example, the more we might complain to each other about how hard it is to get any volunteers for that job, the worse the job sounds, and the harder it is to recruit anyone. We dig ourselves deeper and deeper in trouble.

A negative cycle feels like a trap we cannot escape from. We can get out by starting a positive cycle.

Positive Cycle of Affinity

We can solve the problem of the negative cycle. Because the negative cycle is fueled by our own thoughts and actions, we can use our own thoughts and actions to break out of that cycle. The way to break out of a negative cycle is to start a positive cycle. A positive cycle occurs when positive thinking leads to positive action, and positive action leads to more positive thinking. This is a self-perpetuating cycle, too, only instead of revolving "down, down, down" it rises "up, up, up." Here is an example of a positive cycle to counter the negative cycle of recruitment:

Figure 9D: Positive Cycle of Affinity

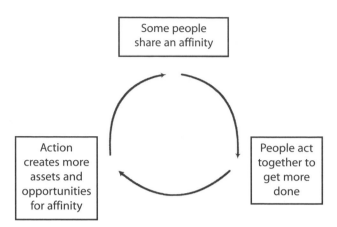

Positive Cycle of Affinity
Two people in the congregation discover that they share a common interest or affinity in some activity. They decide to combine their talents to work together on that activity. Other people see that these two people are having fun, so they want to get involved too, and they see ways to contribute their own talents. With more people involved, the activity becomes more successful, which creates new possibilities for more people to contribute, and the cycle continues.

We have sayings to describe positive cycles like this. "Nothing succeeds like success" is one. "People will get aboard a moving train" is another. I like to use the metaphor of rolling a snowball downhill. The snowball starts with the small clump of snow and grows as you roll it in more snow. The more the snowball rolls, the bigger it gets, and the more momentum it gains.

Where the negative cycle seemed like a hopeless trap, the positive cycle opens up limitless opportunity. This unlimited openness makes the positive cycle a very powerful human dynamic. When we are swept up in a positive cycle, we grow stronger and more confident. We feed off each other's energy. We discover unexpected new opportunities, and we experience renewing power when we take advantage of those opportunities. In the positive cycle of affinity, for example, the shared interests between two people results in successful collaborative action. The action attracts other people and provides an opportunity for them to get involved.

How do we start a positive cycle when we are caught up in a negative one? What changes the human dynamic from one of despair to one of empowerment? Asset mapping provides a framework for making and understanding that shift.

> **CONSULTANT'S JOURNAL**
> ***That's why I love this congregation.***
> *Sunday School was in trouble. My friend had been asked to serve on the education committee and was in the process of making calls to recruit teachers for the next school year. But one call after another, he was being turned down. Even worse, he was discovering that parents who he thought were solid members of the congregation were telling him that they had moved to another congregation.*
>
> *"The bigger church across town has more kids in its program," he told me. "Some of our families moved over there to join the Sunday school. That left fewer kids and parents here, so there was less going on with our Sunday school, so now more families have switched churches. The top leaders from last year's program are telling me they are burned out and need a break from Sunday school responsibilities. What am I going to do?"*
>
> *I asked my friend about his congregations' gifts. He said, "We are a smaller congregation, but that means we are pretty close." I asked him what this gift might have to do with the children. "Well, the adults and the kids in our congregation relate to each other, one-to-one," he said. "This week I saw my younger one sitting at a table with some of the older guys, and they were asking him about summer camp, and talking about their own camp experiences. I thought to myself, that's why I love this congregation." I suggested he share this thought with the people he was calling.*
>
> *Next week I heard from my friend again, and his spirits were much improved. "I decided to take another tack," he said, "and ask people if they would come to a brainstorming meeting about ways to link the skills and talents of adults with young people in our congregation. Even people who had turned me down before agreed to come to that. For the meeting, I went ahead and used that Quick and Simple asset-mapping process you showed me. People got so energized! Now we're looking at doing something completely new and different that will allow adults and young people to get together around things they are interested in. We're going to pull it all together with themes and stories from the Bible. I'm not exactly sure how it's going to work, but we're all walking together on this."*

Open-Sum and Fixed-Sum Dynamics

What drives a cycle around and around? I think that self-perpetuating human cycles are propelled by a way of thinking. In my community experience, I've observed two different ways of thinking that drive two very different cycles.

The first way of thinking is fixed-sum thinking. The fixed-sum idea is this: *your gain comes at my expense* and vice versa. We think we are dividing a fixed pie. The counterpart to this is the open-sum thinking: *your gain is my gain is our gain*. We think we are all contributing to a greater good.

A dynamic is a pattern of interaction between people over time. When people adopt a fixed-sum way of thinking in their dealings with each other, those people together comprise a fixed-sum dynamic. If people adopt an open-sum perspective, those people all make up an open-sum dynamic.

In communities, a fixed-sum dynamic works like a negative cycle. That is, fixed-sum thinking leads people to act, think, and act some more in ways that get worse over time. The opposite happens with open-sum thinking in community. People think and act in ways that strengthen each other to think and act some more.

Fixed-sum thinking: Your gain is my loss.
Open-sum thinking: Your gain is
my gain is our gain.

Consider the example of the negative cycle of recruitment, from above. When we think, "I don't want to get stuck with that job," we are using fixed-sum thinking. We believe that there is a fixed amount of bad work to be done. Your gain (your not having to do the work) comes at my expense (my having to do the work). The fewer the people on the committee, the more work they feel like they are stuck doing. Fixed-sum thinking leads to the action of people walking away from the committee and the task, which leaves the remaining people feeling even more loss from other people's gain, and so on. Fixed-sum thinking propels a self-perpetuating, negative cycle.

The positive cycle of affinity illustrates the connection between open-sum thinking and creating a positive cycle. When we think, "The two of us can accomplish something we care about," we have adopted open-sum thinking. We believe that we both gain when we each get to work on something that matters to us. Your gain (working on something you care about) is my gain (working on something I care about) is our gain (accomplishing something together that we could not accomplish on our own). My action encourages you to act, and your action encourages me to act, and together our action encourages other people to act.

When congregations weaken and leaders burns out, when accusations fly and conflict rules in organizations, when committees and associations have good goals but can't achieve them, when group members are dispirited, cynical, or antagonistic with each other, there is usually a fixed-sum dynamic at work. We sometimes fail to recognize the negative cycles we fall into, and if we do recognize them, we often do not know how to break out of those cycles.

When there is trouble in a congregation,
there is usually a fixed-sum dynamic
at work. But we can break out.

But we can break out. We can reverse the negative dynamics, substituting powerful positive cycles in their place. What results is not just the elimination of the negative, but opening up positive opportunity and action that is as compelling as it is unexpected. This power is easier to experience than to explain. Asset mapping provides a way to experience the power that is in our midst.

Breaking Out with Asset Mapping

Asset mapping works by showing us—or reminding us—how to break out of a negative cycle and into a positive cycle. Asset mapping gives us a framework to identify and use positive, open-sum thinking, which leads to positive action, which renews and strengthens our positive thinking, and so on.

Remember that the open-sum way of thinking is *your gain is my gain is our gain*. Asset mapping engenders this kind of thinking in all three parts of the Quick and Simple Congregational Asset-Mapping Experience: Recognizing Our Assets, Connecting the Dots, and Voting with Our Feet. At each step, something new is created that gives us a common gain. The three elements lead to and grow from each other, modeling an open-sum dynamic. It's a chain of creation.

Figure 9E: A Chain of Creation. Asset mapping models
open-sun dynamics by uncovering new value in each element

	Asset Mapping Elements	New Value	Dynamic
Personal or Individual level	Recognizing Our Assets: Abundance	Renewal: Value in existing assets is lifted up.	Open-sum: Your gain is my gain is our gain.
Small-group level	Connecting the Dots: Affinity	Synergy: Value is found by combining assets.	Open-sum: Your gain is my gain is our gain.
Community level	Voting with Our Feet: Release	Larger Whole: Value of the larger whole emerges from the sum of the parts.	Open-sum: Your gain is my gain is our gain

Recognizing Our Assets

It begins with the half-full cup. Recognizing Our Assets reminds us to focus on the gifts that we have, instead of on our needs or deficiencies. In the process, we *renew* the value of our existing assets.

When we think in terms of our deficiencies, we tend to focus on what other people have that we do not have, what has been lost or taken away, or what we never had in the first place. Because our needs and deficiencies are not useful, we cannot imagine how we might act. As a result, we feel dependent on others to fill our needs, or hopeless at the prospect that they won't. Either way, we are engaged in fixed-sum thinking.

When we see the half-full cup instead of the half-empty cup, we experience a transformation of the mind. Nothing has changed outside of our mind; we are still in exactly the same situation. What has changed is how we think about our situation.

We experience a gain from Recognizing Our Assets. But this gain isn't taken away from someone else. It is newly reclaimed from our own consciousness.

In the Quick and Simple Experience or the Personal Asset Starter, we literally count our blessings. We recognize all the gifts we receive from God, including the assets we overlook or fail to appreciate. Listing our gifts impresses us. We begin to think about *abundance* instead of scarcity. We realize that every need we felt pointed to an asset that we cared about, an asset inside the need. We feel empowered by the experience, because the assets we named can be used to act.

In a sense, what happens in Recognizing Our Assets is the creation of something new through the rediscovery of the old. Like discovering buried treasure, we have found abundant riches in the gifts we already had! It reminds me of Paul's message from Romans 12:2, "Be transformed by the renewing of your minds."

It is this newness, this discovered value, that makes Recognizing Our Assets an open-sum dynamic. We experience a gain from Recognizing Our Assets. But this gain isn't taken away from someone else. It is newly reclaimed from our own consciousness. In the Quick and Simple Experience, for example, we feel support and encouragement for each other as we contribute newly appreciated assets into a pile on our table. We are not tempted to take asset sheets away from someone else! You are happy to affirm my talents. I am only too glad to name some of yours. Together we are uncovering valuable resources. We are acting on the open-sum thinking that your gain is my gain is our gain.

Connecting the Dots

The half-full cup is just the start. When we recognize our own gifts, we realize that we can make things happen by linking assets in new ways. Connecting with other people creates new, shared assets. In this *synergy*, we share a common gain, making Connecting the Dots the second open-sum dynamic in asset mapping.

Negative thinking leads either to negative action or to no action at all. When we think of ourselves as needy and deficient, we compare ourselves to others and think that they have what we do not have. We fence ourselves off from our neighbors to protect our scarce resources against competing needs. We view ourselves in isolation and opposition to others. We are distrustful. We protect "us" from "them." That is fixed-sum thinking.

---

*Affinity is the potential to connect our gifts
and interests with other people
for mutual benefit.*

Something different happens when we relate to other people after experiencing Recognizing Our Assets. First, we realize that if we can uncover the "buried treasure" of our own gifts and interests, then other people have gifts and interests too. Second, we realize that our own gifts are made more valuable by connecting them with other gifts. In the Quick and Simple Experience, for example, our group might figure out that the value of my carpentry skills connect well with your lumber assets to make a table for the sanctuary. Where we once saw scarcity and competition, we now experience abundance and cooperation.

In Connecting the Dots, we seek *affinity* with other people. Affinity is simply the potential to connect our gifts and interests in mutually beneficial ways. Affinity could mean people have *complementary* assets, like my carpentry skills and your lumber for making a table. Affinity also could be found in *similar* interests, like when several bowlers form a bowling team. Affinity does not mean sameness. In fact, some of the greatest potential for collaboration comes between people of diverse assets. Affinity does mean we share a common interest—the interest in linking our existing assets to enjoy something new.

Where the newness we discover in Recognizing Our Assets was a kind of renewal, the newness we find in Connecting the Dots could be described as synergy. We get something new by Connecting our Dots—the table or the bowling team, for example. We both gain from that new asset, so your gain is my gain is our gain, in the open-sum way of thinking. The new asset we create becomes another gift to recognize and connect again (making tables for a furniture shop maybe, or linking bowling teams to form a league?). When we act on our affinities with others, we experience open-sum dynamics.

Voting with Our Feet

Voting with Our Feet is about what happens when we apply open-sum thinking at the community level. Because we have understood and appreciated each other's assets, and because we have seen the affinities we share, we give each other permission to follow our hearts. Releasing control over outcomes, we witness unexpected and amazing things and experience *a good that is larger than all of us.*

No matter how benign our intent, screening inevitably discourages people.

CONSULTANTS' JOURNAL
Yes, we do that—at our other site.
Gulp. I looked out over an audience of more than 1,000 people, gathered from every synod of the 11,000 congregations of the Evangelical Lutheran Church in America. Bishop Hanson asked me to facilitate asset mapping with this group—in 15 minutes. I was honored but apprehensive. I tell everyone that faith in community works every time, right? This would be a test of that confidence.

We asked each person to think about his or her congregation's strengths and assets, then share that with others in small groups and connect the dots. Some volunteered to report their discoveries to the whole gathering.

Juan described himself as a leader of a congregation where services are offered in both Spanish and English. He said that he and the other participants in his small group had discussed ways that their congregations could join in mission partnership with each other. For example, when someone asked a partnering congregation, "Do you have Spanish-language services?" they would say, "Yes we do—at our other site."

I looked down at my notes and I blinked. The next thing I had planned to say was, "When needs become assets, 'they' become 'part of us,' and we become one in the will of God."

The community dynamic builds on the individual and group dynamics we have just discussed. We have seen that negative thinking at the individual and group levels fosters need and distrust. At the community level, that need and distrust leads to denial and controlling behavior. In short, what happens is this: Thinking that resources are scarce, everybody guards against the needs of others, and we struggle over how to cut up the fixed pie. That means we say no to each other a lot.

Eventually, fixed-sum thinking in community leads to a "no" decision. Because our funding is tight, for example, we say no to particular expenditures. Because we have so little available time and attention, we say no to requests for help. This practice has been variously described as gate keeping, priority setting, budgeting, and screening. Whatever the name, it all boils down to saying no to actions. As a result, the community is negating the value or significance of someone's assets. That person hears, "Sorry, your interest got voted down."

No matter how benign our intent, this screening practice discourages people, turns people away, or pushes people out. "If the others aren't interested in my idea," a person will react, "I guess I won't bother going to the meeting." Perhaps they will express their displeasure by dragging their feet or complaining. And every time that happens, our community shrinks in energy and in people. When that happens, we have fewer resources, so we screen more, so we turn more assets away, and we get even smaller. The fixed-sum dynamic destroys community.

When needs become assets, "us and them" becomes "all of us."

There exists an open-sum alternative. The open-sum community dynamic builds on the individual and group levels in a positive way. Recognizing Our Assets leads us to affirm each other's gifts and interests. Connecting the Dots leads us to affirm the contribution of each other's gifts to our common interests. When we create new opportunities we seek affinity with more people, and our circle of affinity grows wider and wider. People who we used to consider outsiders become our brothers and sisters whose contributions are valuable to us. We relate to each other as peers with connectable gifts.

When needs become assets, "us and them" becomes "all of us." We sense that we are in this together. Our own contributions to the collective effort become more meaningful because we know that we are part of something larger and more powerful. At the same time, we release each person to act on his or her call. We trust that we are each building on abundant gifts, opening new affinities, and contributing to the larger good.

What happens next is amazing. People make unexpected connections to accomplish unexpected things. Positive energy grows and multiplies among us! The whole is greater than the sum of its parts!

The whole that is greater than the sum of its parts—that is the third and last witness to creation and open-sum thinking in asset mapping. Like renewal and synergy, this wholeness gives us each a gain that is not taken away from someone else. It is received in common. This wholeness is open-sum. It stirs us to act on the idea that your gain is my gain is our gain.

All three elements of asset mapping manifest open-sum thinking because all lift up or create new value without taking something away. One open-sum dynamic strengthens another, like one snowball adds weight and speed to another snowball. Acting on a sense of abundance strengthens our affinity with others, encouraging us to release each other to act for a larger good, which strengthens our vision of the abundance of God's gifts all over again. Asset mapping models the open-sum dynamic, and that is a very powerful and wonderful experience for us.

Open-Sum Faith, Open-Sum Community

If I get more community, do you get less? Of course not. The idea is ridiculous. If I get more community, you benefit too. If you get more community, I benefit. Together our gains benefit all of our growing and strengthening community. Community is open-sum.

If I get more faith, do you get less? No, that is silly too. My faith does not come out of your supply. In fact, if I get more faith, that can actually strengthen your faith. And together, our growing faith can only further strengthen the faith of others. Faith is open-sum.

Faith and community are open-sum, and asset mapping models open-sum dynamics. I think this is why asset mapping strengthens faith and community. Asset mapping is a demonstration of the powerful open-sum dynamics within faith and community, and it is a tool for tapping that power.

Fixed-sum dynamics do not go with community. I said earlier that community is voluntary and self-identifying. You cannot force someone to join a community. When we try to control the contributions of others, they become discouraged. Control dissipates the energy needed for collective effort. In community, the fixed-sum approach is self-defeating. I tell people, you cannot make a snowball with a screen!

Fixed-sum dynamics do not go with faith either. The mindsets of scarcity, and mistrust, and control just do not work. Faith is personal. We each struggle with what faith means to us, but we do know that faith lives within us. It cannot be screened or allocated by another. Can you imagine members of the prayer chain saying, "Sorry, we've used up all our faith today. We cannot pray for you. Try again tomorrow"?

The open-sum power of faith and community is something we feel from the heart. Lessons of faith and community go together and grow stronger through experience. We feel that power when we look at our half-full cup, which reminds us of God's abundance and strengthens our faith that we are all God's children with something to contribute. Without spelling it out, we can sense the open-sum power of those ideas together.

"Love thy neighbor" is a pillar of our faith. Connecting the dots points to the affinities we share with each other. As we make new things happen together, we feel the power of faith in our daily lives.

In community we realize that we are all part of something bigger. We do not have to be convinced that we are one in God. We feel this connection when allow each person to follow his or her heart. We experience it when we witness unexpected and wonderful gifts.

Placing ourselves in God's hands, faith and community opens up to us. To me, asset mapping feels like the Spirit moving within the room. In the newness of abundance, affinity, and release, we discover a presence in our midst. There is something in the space between us that we witness when we make a faithful, loving community together. It feels like grace, moving between our gifts.

Chapter 10

Frequently Shared Lessons

THE BEAUTIFUL THING about the Quick and Simple Asset-Mapping Experience is that you can just go through the experience and feel it work. You will be led by the open-sum dynamics of asset mapping. Learn from that and do it some more.

I am part of a growing network of people who are sharing what we learn from building assets in communities of faith. We are not trying to establish one formal system or procedure. We do pass along tips, techniques for getting things done, and lessons for steering away from traps and dead ends. I invite you to share the lessons you learn with others, to contribute to our larger community. In that same spirit, I share the lessons I have learned with you.

Internet Web sites often have a useful section called "Frequently Asked Questions," or FAQs for short. In asset mapping, no one person has all the answers. We all have something to share, and something to learn. So let's coin a new term and call these "Frequently Shared Lessons," or FSLs.

WHAT CONGREGATIONAL
ASSET MAPPING IS, AND IS NOT

Question: *What is congregational asset mapping, exactly? What can we use it for?*
Frequently Shared Lesson: Congregational asset mapping is power for faith in community.

Asset mapping is a practical tool. It can be used for getting unstuck, renewing faith, making things happen, discovering mission, spreading the word, and widening our circle of community. In that sense, congregational asset mapping could be described as a *tool* to support planning, relationship building, conflict resolution, project development, problem solving, partnership negotiation, stewardship, evangelism, worship, and congregational growth.

Congregational asset mapping is also a *mind-set*. It is an open-sum way of thinking that sparks, nurtures, and renews mission. The process reminds us of God's abundant gifts, our untapped affinities with each other, and the unexpected power of release that we experience when we turn control over to God.

---

*Congregational asset mapping is power
for faith in community.*

The Quick and Simple Congregational Asset-Mapping Experience provides an easy way for groups of people to experience the power of faith in community. Congregational asset mapping gives us both a framework and a language to understand each other. Though the process, language, and framework of asset mapping may be new to us, the idea is not. Asset mapping affirms what we already know about abundance, affinity, and release because we have practiced our faith and participated in community. Congregational asset mapping encourages us to appreciate our own experience, share it, celebrate it, and do it all some more.

In that sense, the power of congregational asset mapping is more than a practical tool or a mind-set. It is permission. Congregational asset mapping gives us permission to apply what we know to what we care about in our lives.

Q: *Is congregational asset mapping a program?*
FSL: No, congregational asset mapping is not a program. It is not a system, a formal method, or a packaged plan to follow and get right. There is no right way of doing asset mapping; there are no proper procedures to follow; and there are no certain steps to take. Asset mapping is as individual as you are and as unique as your call in your ever-widening community.

The Quick and Simple Congregational Asset-Mapping Experience *is* a process, and it does have steps, and there are good practices to follow that help make it work. (Plus, it only takes an hour!) The Quick and Simple Experience is not supposed to be "the right way to do congregational asset mapping." It is

---

Congregational Asset Mapping is:
- A practical tool for action
- A mindset and an affirmation
- A permission

---

just one way of building on assets. By experiencing asset mapping in the Quick and Simple Experience, we can learn by doing, and apply what we learn to our own situations.

> **Q:** *Is congregational asset mapping the same as optimism?*
> **FSL:** No, I don't see it that way. There is a difference between optimism and using our gifts to discover and embrace God's plan for us.

Carol R. Smith, a trainer with the National Catholic Rural Life Conference, says asset mapping is not optimism; it is hard-core pragmatism. We have to do it to get things done. What else can we do but use what we have got to get what we want?

The old blues lyric goes, "You can't use what you ain't got." We cannot do anything with needs and deficits. We can act out of our combined assets. Asset mapping is empowering and hopeful, but it is not wishful thinking. It is what we can do, nothing more, and thankfully, nothing less.

> **Q:** *Is congregational asset mapping the same as bootstrapping?*
> **FSL:** No, asset mapping is not about leaving each other to our own devices. On the contrary, relationships are central to asset mapping.

Bootstrapping is short for, "Lift yourself up by your own bootstraps." It's an ironic way of saying, "Do it yourself," because we cannot literally lift ourselves up by our own bootstraps. In asset mapping, we do take responsibility for ourselves, our gifts, and our congregation. Asset mapping starts by recognizing and appreciating our own gifts, including our bootstraps. But that's just the start, because our gifts can't do anything by themselves. Recognizing our assets leads us to identify our affinities with other people and build relationships, so that we can unleash the power of faith in community.

In other contexts, however, I have heard the term "bootstrapping" used with pride by people who are describing their own efforts to build communities of faith from the bottom up. For example, local residents who are planting their own church by using their collective assets to leverage other resources might say they are "bootstrapping." In that sense, asset mapping is very much like bootstrapping.

> **Asset Mapping is NOT:**
> - A program
> - Simple optimism
> - Bootstrapping

Recapping Lessons from the Quick and Simple Experience

Q: *Who is congregational asset mapping for? What kinds of people are best for the process?*

FSL: It takes all types of people to build community. Watch and listen to participants in the Quick and Simple Congregational Asset-Mapping Experience. Some express validation and freedom. Others talk about new insight and perspective. Together, people of all types seem empowered to support each other in their calls.

Maybe you have heard of personality tests that categorize personal behavior in order to support us in understanding one another. These can compliment the asset-mapping process by reminding us that we each bring unique and valuable gifts to the community. But whatever our personality types, faith and community are open-sum dynamics. Asset mapping models open-sum dynamics for us, so we can apply our own styles and talents for the larger good.

CONSULTANT'S JOURNAL

She's a faithful type of person.

A president of a church council told me that she wasn't an open-process type of person. "I appreciate what the Quick and Simple Experience may do for others," she said, "but it seems so open-ended. I still need order and control."

I reflected on what she had done as a congregational leader. She had instituted prayer and devotions in council meetings. She had worked behind the scenes to match up people with complementary skills and interests for new ministries. She used her orderly mind to structure meetings so that people with diverse gifts could contribute. She did what she could do as a faithful person working in community.

In the middle of a lake, we are all swimming-type of people. Except for any one who walks on the water, that is.

Q: *What kind of resistance might I get from potential participants? What can I do about it?*

FSL: People may have preconceived notions about what will happen. Move participants into the process quickly, so that they can experience it for themselves. Do not worry too much about the people who do not show up. Work with whomever you get. Do not worry about participants who are anxious or doubtful. The process will sell them—you don't have to!

Some people do not like organized group process of any kind. Maybe they have had bad experiences with exercises that seem pointless or corny. Maybe they are reserved about showing feelings and expressing ideas. Other people prefer not to lose center stage to a democratic group process.

Whatever the reason, you can let the Quick and Simple Experience speak for itself. I have seen reluctant and resistant people completely turn around once they get into the process. Spend as little time as possible introducing the process and begin.

If someone does not want to attend, they won't. That is Voting with Their Feet, right? Don't worry about it; you don't need a majority or a quorum to proceed. Work with who is there. It only takes a small clump of snow to start a snowball. As the snowball grows, other people will find ways to join.

CONSULTANT'S JOURNAL

Yes, we really are going to do something positive.

One guy kept complaining about the process. "I'm pretty negative, I know," he said. Then later, "Oh no, you're not going to make me write down my own gifts!" Then, "Do we all have to stand up and go to the wall?" He wasn't trying to be mean. It was just his reaction. I kept smiling at him, joking with him, and moving the process along.

The next day the man called me on the phone to tell me how much he had gotten out of the experience, and more importantly, how excited he was about the actions of the group. He said, "I'm so excited that we are going to enable people to act on the things they really care about."

Q: *What are the most important keys for facilitating the Quick and Simple Experience?*
FSL: People get excited about opening up possibilities. They enjoy discovering new assets, new affinities, and a whole that is greater than the sum of its parts. Any dead ends come from the intrusion of fixed-sum dynamics into an open-sum process.

Let's recap the key lessons for facilitating the Quick and Simple Congregational Asset-Mapping Experience.

- *Tap into your own affinity for the group you're facilitating.*
  Find an interest that you share with the people you are working with. Maybe you are part of the same group, congregation, district, or denomination. Perhaps you are from the same neighborhood, state, or part of the country. Or you might identify with the challenges the group faces or the way they get things done. Use this affinity to consider yourself a

colleague of the group and not an outsider. Then you can approach the session as a collective effort and see your facilitation as part of a larger movement to share and inspire open-sum community building.

- *Uncover buried treasure, not a priority list.*
  In Recognizing Our Assets, rounds of focus questions and sharing in groups will reveal overlooked and unappreciated gifts. All that affirmation will raise the spirits in the room! Steer clear of fixed-sum thinking by reminding participants that this is not a complete catalog or even a priority list, just a sample of gifts that they thought of in this particular session.

- *Brainstorm actions, not categories.*
  In Connecting the Dots, participants use affinities to brainstorm new collaborative actions. Steer clear of fixed-sum dynamics by reminding participants not to put assets into categories. When we categorize assets, we limit the creative actions that emerge from mixing different types of assets.

- *Look around.*
  In Voting with Our Feet, participants glimpse the whole that is greater than the sum of the parts and they love it. It will not be necessary to steer clear of fixed-sum dynamics. The real fun comes when you ask participants to look around, and they begin to reflect on what they have done.

- *Open up reflection.*
  What you have experienced as a group is a model of open-sum dynamics in faith and community. Participatory group discussion should open up reflection on this open-sum process. Steer clear of closure. Watch for unexpected lessons and applications to appear over time in your community of faith.

Q: *What do we do if someone is stuck on needs and deficits?*
FSL: Resist the temptation to return the negativity. Instead, affirm the person. Use their negative statements as an opportunity to show the assets inside the need, using the needs transformation exercise described in chapter 5. And you might be surprised! Often, other participants will do this naturally. You may invite this process by asking, "Can anyone help?"

I have made mistakes on this one. I have told the person, "Now, you're being negative. You know we're trying to focus on assets here." Some people might be helped by that corrective, but a person stuck on negatives hears it as additional criticism. It actually feeds one's tendency to focus on needs because the individual feels that he or she has to explain the need and deficiency even more strongly.

Whenever this has happened to me, I have been rescued by group participants. Other group members have affirmed the person's gifts and strengths. They have found ways to connect them with other assets. I learned to do that myself, the next time.

CONSULTANT'S JOURNAL

Your daughter is an asset to us.

We were going around the group, reading to each other from the assets we had recognized. We got to Renee, and she started to present ways to fill needs instead of build on assets. She was talking about her daughter, Sarah, who gets around in a wheelchair.

I smiled and said, "Remember we're focusing on assets here." She didn't object but she got quiet. I knew I had rubbed her the wrong way. I asked the group, "Can anybody help here?"

One woman said, "Renee, your daughter is an asset to us. I still remember the day we worked together on that ramp to the front door. That was the day our congregation really started thinking about the different skills and perspectives we each have.

"And without Sarah, I know my children wouldn't be in Sunday school. She's the one always talking to them about church.

"The question I have, Renee, is, how we can build on Sarah's gifts to strengthen our congregation even further? How can we use Sarah's gifts with all these other gifts we've identified to accomplish things we care about?"

That's when Renee seemed to rejoin the group. She just smiled and said, "Well, you know, I do have an idea."

STRATEGY FOR OPEN-SUM ACTION

Q: *But what if people vote with their feet and something important gets left out? How do I know that people will do what they "should" do?*
FSL: You don't know what people will do. You can have faith that what "should" be done, will be done.

Frankly, it's a little scary to release control over outcomes. What if people keep doing what they have always done? What if no one volunteers for the basic things we need to do for survival? What if people stay in their little groups and do not reach out to others? What if the actions we take on do not seem to accomplish our mission? What if no one acts at all?

Believe me, I know those feelings. I feel some of that anxiety every time I facilitate the Quick and Simple Experience. Do you know what? The asset mapping always works. I have witnessed amazing gains, beyond my own expectations.

I do not think this happens because of the Quick and Simple Experience. I think it happens because of faith and community. Asset mapping simply models the open-sum dynamic in faith and community.

Have faith in your own community to do what they should do. When you see what happens, you will realize you did not accomplish anything. You witnessed something, something that feels like grace.

CONSULTANT'S JOURNAL
Now it looks like mission.

I met with a group of clergy and congregational leaders to talk about their experiences with asset mapping. It had been six months or so since their congregations had each gone through an early version of the Quick and Simple Experience.

Cheri, a pastor with an urban congregation said, "Our congregation has been down in the dumps. The last thing I wanted to see was more work for us. Since the asset mapping, our new ideas for mission have gotten people more involved. Now people have been taking responsibilities off of my shoulders. I didn't realize it, but I was burned out. With renewed leadership, now I'm thinking I might be able to take a sabbatical."

Phil, a suburban congregational leader said, "We went into asset mapping thinking that we were landlocked, because we are located on a stretch of land between the airport and the ocean. The ministries we developed have drawn lots of new people, including many Spanish-speaking folks and recent immigrants. We're not landlocked, we are centrally located for our new sense of mission."

Von, one of the rural leaders said, "We were shrinking so much we thought about survival more than anything else. Asset mapping led us to recognize that we are an important part of our larger rural community. Now we are partnering with the local school district and running a successful after-school program. We're focused on the strengths of our people, and the strength of our congregation is following right along."

Tim, the exurban pastor said, "Our congregation is so new, we still tended to think of ourselves as somebody else's mission. Raising money for a building expansion just didn't seem possible, so we didn't focus on that in the asset mapping. Since then, people have gotten involved and taken up leadership. Now the building expansion doesn't look like fundraising, it looks like our own mission."

Q: *Can we apply asset mapping to an existing project or mission?*
FSL: Absolutely. You might think of three ways to apply asset mapping:

- Targeted asset mapping: To mobilize people for action on a project you've already agreed on.
- Visionary asset mapping: To discover community vision and mission, by working backwards from the actions and affinities that people create together.
- Asset mapping for connections: To build groups of people around affinities, instead of trying to recruit people to jobs they do not want to do.

There will more on these applications in chapter 11.

Q: *Can we hedge our bets, and look at BOTH assets and needs?*
FSL: You cannot do asset mapping partway. The whole point is openness. But, you can start small.

It does not matter how many people start asset mapping together. A snowball starts with a small clump of snow. You can start asset mapping with five people or five thousand. It does not matter how many assets participants recognize. Participants can apply asset mapping to any size project and it will still be effective. If people recognize and build on assets, by connecting them with each other and voting with their feet, they will set up an open-sum process that will grow over time.

If you try to mix fixed-sum methods into the open-sum process, you will close down the open-sum process and it will lose its power. Remember, fixed-sum dynamics narrow down choices and deny participant's interests. Think of fixed-sum dynamics as a box and open-sum dynamics as blue sky. You cannot put blue sky inside a box! Even a small hole in the box will let you peek out to the blue sky above. Asset mapping will work as long as it is unlimited. If you want to hedge your bets, start small but don't mix assets and needs.

Consider a funder I met who wanted to empower youth as grantmakers. The funder set up a program, a fund, and selected a youth committee to make grants based on assets. The monies were to be spent according to guidelines set by the funder, and all grant decisions had to be approved by the funder. The funder still said no to the youth when it counted. The funder had created a fixed-sum dynamic.

Now consider a congregation I met that set up a small-grants project to spark new ministries. They established a fund and announced that any group of five people or more, who committed to together to work on a ministry of shared interest, could receive a grant of up to $500 for that project. No strings attached. The fund was small, and eventually the money ran out. Still, the effort started a snowball of ministries in the congregation. It is better to start a small open-sum effort like this than a larger effort that's really fixed-sum.

> **Q:** *What if we believe that other people are thinking and acting in a fixed-sum way? Can we tell them to do asset mapping?*
> **FSL:** Community is voluntary. People do congregational asset mapping because they want to strengthen faith and community. You cannot tell someone else to do that. But you can use a carrot instead of a stick by providing opportunities for people to use their gifts

Asset mapping changes the way we see things. If we see the frustrations of other people locked in fixed-sum dynamics, we want to provide a solution. If we say, "You people should do asset mapping," it can sound like we are deprecating their talents and skills instead of lifting them up.

Show other people that asset mapping works by doing it with people who are already willing and interested. Perhaps the group locked in a fixed-sum dynamic connects with another group you participate in. Offer the Quick and Simple Experience as a non-threatening, one-hour, low-cost option to those groups. (For advice on opportunities to approach this, see chapter 3.) The message will spread as projects take root and energy builds. The best part is, you will be building on your own assets, without wasting energy worrying about what other people won't do.

> **Q:** *What if we want to take action, and the powers that be still say no? What if "they" won't let us do what we feel called to do?*
> **FSL:** Use the assets you *do* control to get things done. The actions you take will create a powerful, growing snowball of faithful, community effort. You will show the powers that be a successful alternative to fixed-sum thinking. You will also develop assets and relationships that build community leadership and accountability.

Hear this carefully. I am not suggesting that you give up the interests that you have in institutional or community assets, nor am I suggesting you start some unnecessary conflict with the powers that be. On the contrary, I am suggesting that when groups of people build on their assets, accountable leadership is strengthened as faith and community relationships grow.

Most of the time, I find that leaders of faith communities are enthusiastic about asset mapping in the first place. The idea and the approach seem to cut across political, economic, and social lines. You might be surprised at the response you get from the powers that be, both for the process and for the mission-driven actions that you take up.

But of course, "they" might say no to something. We all know that leaders are faced with pressures around budgets, time, and space and other resources that often seem scarce or fixed-sum. In a fixed-sum dynamic, we say *no* to each other.

The way to get out of that is by saying *yes* to each other, starting with the circle of folks we know who recognize some common interests. We can share our faith with each other without asking permission of a church council, for example. We can discover affinities and connect our gifts to make things happen with or without a grant from the denomination. When we say yes to each other, we begin or renew an open-sum dynamic that strengthens faith and community.

What do the powers that be think about all this? They are usually amazed and thrilled! Positive things are happening that they did not have to force from the top down. Energy and success are coming from the ground up, strengthening the community and making the leaders look good as a result. Usually, I see that the powers that be want to get on board the moving train and take advantage of the new opportunities we have created. They will match funding, or share resources, to connect the dots between the assets they control and the gifts and energy lifted up by the community.

A funder, for example, would rather contribute a critical piece of support to a project that already has energy, participation, and local assets behind it, than make a grant to a project that is all need and no assets. Funders call that leverage. The more asset building we do, the easier job our leaders have.

And if the powers that be still say no?

- First, you still have your widening circle of people taking action together. You are better off than you were before.
- Second, you will be growing a web of mutual relationships between people, so that makes a strong constituency to hold leaders accountable.
- Third, you are developing capable and faithful new leaders throughout that web of people. The people involved with you are developing trust and understanding with each other, and witnessing the success of open-sum dynamics. People who have been through asset mapping often rise to successful leadership, because they see the bigger picture, and appreciate the contributions of each person to the larger good.

CONSULTANT'S JOURNAL
The people who said yes to no.
I learned about saying yes *in a community where people got told* no *a lot. Bethel Lutheran Church is in West Garfield Park on Chicago's West Side. The*

congregation was told no by white flight in the 1960s and '70s, and told no by the riots following Martin Luther King, Jr.'s assassination. You could not borrow money to buy or fix up a home in the community because the banks and insurance companies redlined the area as a no-loan area strictly on the basis of race.

The congregation said yes anyway. They looked at their gifts, mortgaged the church, and pooled their personal credit cards to cover the costs. With hard work and prayer, they rehabilitated a dilapidated two-flat into a decent home for two families, and created a sign of hope for everyone. They said yes to themselves, yes to each other, and yes to God.

That act started a snowball of development. With a real housing development under its belt, the church created a nonprofit community development corporation called Bethel New Life, led by Dr. Mary Nelson, a brilliant and faithful asset thinker who inspired me. By the time I came to work there, Bethel New Life was developing dozens of housing units and branching into economic development.

At the same time, organized residents of disinvested communities around the country were pushing for and winning national legislation to stop the redlining that was devastating communities like West Garfield Park. The Community Reinvestment Act required banks to reinvest loan monies in communities where they received bank deposits.

As community representatives, we sat at the negotiating table with the leaders of very large banks, the ones who had been saying no for all those years. The negotiations depended upon the experience and capability of organizations like Bethel, who had been making affordable housing work without the help of developers. The banks agreed to reinvest hundreds of millions of dollars.

A funny thing happened. The banks made a decent profit on their loans in the inner city. Those loans were not bad risks after all. It took the different gifts of community residents, banks, organizers, and developers to reverse the negative cycle of disinvestment and begin a positive cycle of neighborhood development. Together we accomplished something none of us could accomplish on our own.

When the Community Reinvestment Act came up for renewal five years later, the community residents and the bank leaders went to Congress together. This time, the banks said, "Yes."

AFTER THE QUICK AND SIMPLE EXPERIENCE

Q: *What's the next step after the Quick and Simple Congregational Asset-Mapping Experience?*
FSL: The next step is to stop taking steps. The idea is to move, over time, from asset mapping to asset thinking to opening up our hearts and minds

to God in all things. There are mechanisms and vehicles that congregations and communities have set up to encourage and support open-sum action over time. But ultimately, asset mapping is about how we live our lives in community.

A remarkable thing about the Quick and Simple Experience is how easily people learn to facilitate the process. After spending an hour or so on the process one day, I ask participants to facilitate the process with new people the next day. This book can help guide you and give you confidence to do just that.

Make the snowball grow by sharing asset mapping with people you know and encouraging them to do the same. The more that people in your widening community create and share assets, the more opportunities there will be for everybody. Celebrate your progress together, and do it some more.

Lose the markers, tape, and pens,
and simply approach each other
in community through faith.

Because the Quick and Simple Experience can be used in a number of ways, you may certainly wish to reuse the process with a particular group. For instance, if the Quick and Simple Experience worked as an ice-breaker and visioning process, you could try it again later to implement a particular project or to widen your circle of people working in community.

But do not make the Quick and Simple Experience into a formal program. Instead, you'll end up losing the markers, tape, and pens and simply approaching each other in community through faith.

Very often, congregations and communities of faith set up ongoing vehicles for recognizing assets, connecting the dots, and voting with our feet. We might call these engines for open-sum action, clearinghouses, resource centers, network servers, or any number of names. Whatever the name, these vehicles aim to make building on assets an ongoing way of working and renewing faith. These vehicles incorporate the elements of asset mapping into their community life, to:

- *Create welcoming situations, where people are encouraged to recognize and share gifts.*
 Gifts could be shared in regularly scheduled open gatherings, in newsletters, or online discussions.

114

- *Open opportunities for people to identify affinities with each other to make new things happen.*
  This could happen by providing networking time at a regular gathering when new teams identified or by providing space for self initiated group activities.

- *Affirm and give permission to people to follow their hearts in wider circles of faith and community.*
  Congregations gather to share stories of actions that have been taken and then brainstorm additional connections and supports. Stories could also be shared in a newsletter or online forum.

Some of the simplest versions of open-sum engines are familiar to all of us. A regularly scheduled potluck supper or covered-dish meal is an open-sum way to feed ourselves. If you think about it, all kinds of mutual aid and peer support groups are open-sum engines because they bring us together to share gifts in an open way. In the process, the experience creates something bigger.

Some congregations have dedicated existing committees or groups to building on assets. Virtually any group in or around a congregation could function this way, from the stewardship committee to a Bible study group, from a youth council to the board of directors of the endowment. I have seen congregations manage their governing council around asset mapping to great success. Engines for open-sum action often work outside a traditional congregational structure as well. Coalitions of congregations or community groups, for example, usually facilitate the sharing of lessons and the opening of opportunities for collaboration.

One caution: when budgets and staff grow, fixed-sum thinking tends to take root. All too often voluntary groups that start out vibrant and active fall off when group attention shifts toward obtaining funding and supervising personnel. Some well-funded and staffed ministries are strongly focused on open-sum asset building, but getting and keeping money puts challenging fixed-sum pressures on a start-up ministry. Personally, I would recommend that you stay away from seeking outside grants and contracts until you have built up strong group habits for open-sum thinking and action.

CONSULTANT'S JOURNAL

What else can we do?

After living in the inner city all my life, I moved to a small town in rural Iowa when my wife got a new job. They say God closes a door and opens a window, and that's how I felt as I received the opportunity to visit with and work for grassroots community organizations doing amazing things in small-town and rural areas around the nation.

It seems to me that building on assets is a way of life to most rural communities. We have always had to use what we've got, to get what we want. It is not surprising, then, that some of my most inspiring asset-building experiences have been with rural folks. As an example of what an engine for open-sum action might look like, I often talk about the people I met from the Newton County Resource Council in the Ozark Mountains of Arkansas.

The council was composed of a somewhat unusual combination of community leaders. They realized from the start that they would not get much done on their own. They invited anyone who had an idea for the community to come share it at any of their regular gatherings. They did not evaluate or screen ideas. They just listened and looked for chances to make connections. Someone had an idea for a tourist information booth, and someone else had an idea to sell locally made arts and crafts. They put these two assets together with an unused property near the entrance to town and created a shop that drew tourists to the artwork. The shop was cooperatively staffed by the artisans.

The council ended up working as a kind of network and incubator for community ideas. The council meetings enabled people to make connections to start or strengthen projects. The organization would provide a home for a project if necessary to get it off the ground but spin it off as an independent organization as soon as possible. That way the council stayed small even as it helped develop a wide range of initiatives to strengthen the community, including a women's shelter, a housing development organization, a recycling center, an Internet service provider, and a mountaintop recreational trail system.

Congregational asset mapping could result in ministries like these or in very different expressions of mission. What I learned from Newton County goes for any faith community: We can only get where we want to go by strengthening each other. That is not an exercise or a process; it's a way of life.

Chapter 11

More Frequently
Shared Lessons

Congregational Life

THIS CHAPTER OFFERS Frequently Shared Lessons on the uses of asset mapping in important aspects of congregational life, including stewardship, congregational development, faith partnerships, leadership in public life, and evangelism. Congregations find that the open-sum power demonstrated by asset mapping resonates with these efforts in important ways.

STEWARDSHIP

Q: *What about money? How can we use asset mapping to enhance our fundraising efforts?*
FSL: Asset mapping is not a fundraising program or system. It provides powerful support for stewardship. People learn to share their gifts with each other. People gain a richer understanding of themselves as givers and stewards. As a result, congregations grow in stewardship and fundraising.

Many congregations and communities of faith do an excellent job with fundraising. The formal fundraising programs I have seen place congregational finances in the larger context of faith, witness, and stewardship. Asset mapping makes that context tangible for participants, puts it in practice, and shows how stewardship renews our resources and opens our hearts.

We tend to think of money in a fixed-sum way. That is, your financial gain comes at my financial expense. In community, this mind-set leads to a negative cycle, an ever-shrinking fixed-sum dynamic. Thinking that money is scarce, we

Figure 11A: Negative Cycle of Scarcity in Fundraising

```
        ┌─────────────────┐
        │  Money appears  │
        │     scarce.     │
        └─────────────────┘

                  Negative
                   Cycle of
                  Scarcity
                in Fundraising

┌──────────────┐              ┌──────────────┐
│ We have less │              │  We act to   │
│    money to  │              │  protect our │
│   support    │              │  money from  │
│ congregation │              │  competing   │
│ and ministry.│              │    needs.    │
└──────────────┘              └──────────────┘
```

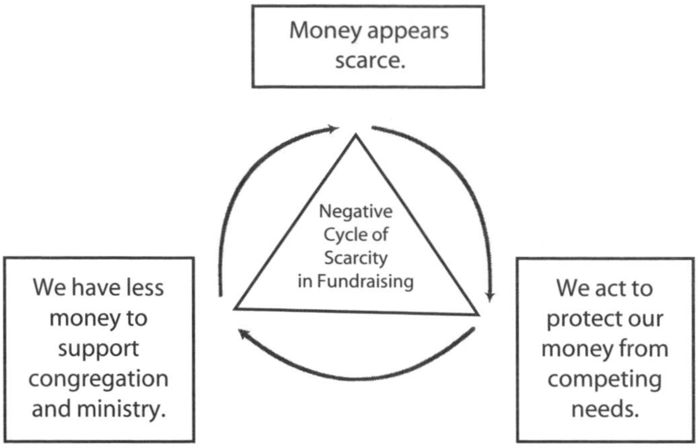

protect, allocate, and gatekeep our supply. We end up denying each other. So we withdraw or walk away, which leaves fewer resources, and on it goes.

We try to reflect a different approach in communities of faith. We give thanks for our gifts and return them to God. When we share our gifts, we do so willingly. We seek a larger good than our narrow self-interest. In short, we open ourselves to God's will.

How do we share our faith without telling each other what to do? Asset mapping offers a way for us to model a positive cycle of stewardship, drawing on the open-sum way of thinking. We recognize and are thankful for abundant gifts, we share these gifts in action with others, and together we share even larger and ever-growing blessings in community.

With asset mapping, we experience stewardship in action in our community.

Stewardship is open-sum: Your gain is my gain is our gain. Whether or not we focus specifically on stewardship, The Quick and Simple Congregational Asset-Mapping Experience gives us a way to participate in this open-sum dynamic. People in any asset-mapping effort learn lessons crucial to stewardship, including:

- *Stewardship is active.*
  Connecting the Dots and Voting with Our Feet shows us that the value of our gifts is released when we share them with other people. Because we are blessed with abundant gifts, we are compelled to act generously.

Figure 11B: Positive Cycle of Abundance in Stewardship

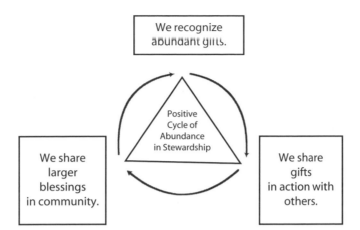

- *Stewardship goes beyond money.*
  Money is only one kind of gift. We have many gifts, more than we recognize. We can get things done by connecting our gifts as part of a larger community of faith. With that growing faith, giving grows, and money is recycled and multiplied.

- *Stewardship generates continuous renewal.*
  In each element of asset mapping, we witness the creation of new value and assets. Together, we get things done that we could not get done on our own. The unexpected happens, and we are amazed. We experience God's blessings, not as a narrow bargain for favors returned, but as a continuous renewal of faith in community.

CONSULTANT'S JOURNAL
A congregation discovers its stewardship committee.
I had a chance to sit down with a minister and a lay leader from a suburban congregation about a year after they had attended an asset-mapping workshop I facilitated. In conversation, I learned that their congregational giving had increased 50 percent that year. I asked what happened, and Tanya and Yung Mi told me a story about how they discovered their stewardship committee.

"I gave up on even having a stewardship committee," said Tanya, the minister. "Every year was worse than the year before. The committee members would have a terrible time getting participation in the fall fundraising campaign. People acted as though their giving was a favor to the committee or to me. Committee members quit, and nobody would volunteer, because they

saw what had happened to the previous committees. We've had to do without any campaign."

Then Yung Mi, the lay leader, said, "I never gave stewardship a thought, really. But I was turned on by the idea of asset mapping, because it made me feel like I could do something right away. I knew some other people who liked to garden, so we connected the dots. We joined up with the property committee and started to grow vegetables around the church. Some of the gardeners were involved with the Boys and Girls Club, and the youth saw an opportunity to raise money for their field trip by growing and selling vegetables. They started meeting at the church. Those meetings gave other groups the idea. Now we have something going on in the building just about every night.

Tanya chimed in, "Yes, I think that's how the worship committee got involved in the new day care center. A group of parents were pushing for child care during services. They thought about all the unused space we have during weekdays. Two members were taking in kids at home, so this seemed like a good opportunity for them to branch out."

I told the two leaders that this sounded great. "But," I asked, "what does all this have to do with a stewardship committee?"

"That's the thing," said Tanya. "There's so much going on, and we keep finding new connections to make things happen. Everybody is helping each other out or piggybacking one thing with another. We have worked together on lots of little fundraisers to fill in the gaps. One day we had a gathering of a bunch of the leaders to share our news and plans and ideas. Somebody said we should meet regularly. Somebody else said, 'Right, and we should cooperate on a larger fundraising campaign to save time. And that's when I stood up," the minister said, "and said I think we just discovered our stewardship committee."

People learn by doing. Asset mapping gives your congregation a way to experience stewardship in action. That is permission enough. People will run with it and take the congregation to places no one can predict.

Congregational Development

Q: *We're having a hard time recruiting volunteers for some critical congregational tasks. Can asset mapping help?*
FSL: Yes! An extraordinary strength of asset mapping is that it helps us understand how and why volunteers work together in community. What we learn is *not* to recruit people to tasks they do not want to do. Instead, we learn to gather and organize people around their affinities with each other. We call that *asset mapping for connections.*

Congregations and communities of faith are voluntary. When we try to coerce people into work, it only frustrates people. Involuntary volunteers will do a poor job, feel bad about it, and walk away. They will vote with their feet, whether you ask them to or not.

On the other hand, people whose gifts are affirmed and whose interests are engaged will contribute far more than we expect. When we feel ourselves a part of something bigger, we actually seek and find ways to apply our gifts in new ways. Work does not feel like sacrifice; it feels like participating in a larger good.

When community strengthens our faith, we put our faith in community.

Let's say you ask a friend to join the property committee, and he agrees. Every time you call him about a meeting, he says he has to go fishing. You could fault him for his insincerity and criticize his priorities. You could also note your friend's gifts and interests and talk to him about leading a fishing trip.

What does fishing got to do with anything? You could connect a fishing trip to a study of any one of the many Bible stories about fish. Of course, the real power in this idea comes from affirmation and affinity. Your friend enjoys going fishing with people he cares about, and now he sees his congregation as a place where he can do that. When your friend cares about his congregation, there is nothing he will not do. Community strengthens his faith, so he puts his faith in community.

But what about the critical tasks—worship preparation, fundraising, administration, and so forth? Can we rely on affinity for that? The critical tasks will get done when people follow their hearts. People will step up to the work at hand when they feel they are a part of a larger group acting in their collective interests. When you connect the dots, you also may discover that the critical tasks are not what you thought they were.

Remember, affinity is not sameness. It is the common interest that we share when we connect our gifts to get things done..

Remember, affinity is not sameness. It is the common interest that we share when we connect our gifts to get things done. Often, the greatest affinities are between dissimilar gifts. For example, you might have a friend who does not like meetings, but he is great with kids and might be happy to watch the children during the meeting so that others can attend. *Asset mapping for connections* gives people an opportunity to knit together their gifts with the gifts of others.

121

CONSULTANT'S JOURNAL
They'd rather be out on the water.
Some leaders from congregations in a lake resort area were talking about what it is like to hold worship services there in the summer. As you can imagine, many people said that they would rather be out on the lake, boating.

So the congregation arranged to hold services on the lake! They invited people with boats to meet at a certain spot, tied up together, and they conducted services on the water. Boaters would invite non-boaters to ride in their boats, building new relationships within the congregations. Unchurched boaters were intrigued by the strange flotilla they saw on the lake. They said, "Any church that will come this far, I've got to check out." Soon, many of the unchurched boaters had joined and become active members.

Q: *How can we use asset mapping to implement a project we are already committed to doing? Can we build on assets even if we have planned on needs?*
FSL: Absolutely. It is never too late to build on your assets. Asset mapping makes an excellent tool for getting unstuck or making a project happen. Just be careful to avoid the dead ends that can put you right back into a needs-based, fixed-sum approach.

To use assets to implement a project, use the Quick and Simple Experience and apply it to your project goals and directions. This is what I call *targeted asset mapping*. For example, if you are revitalizing your Bible study group, when you Connect the Dots, ask participants to "connect the dots to revitalize the Bible Study group in mission." It is that easy.

As committee or group members Connect the Dots to get things done, they will have to seek out other people who have the assets that complement their own. Members will learn something about other people's interests, in order to engage those people in joint action. The circles of people involved in the committee's efforts will grow wider and wider.

What do we gain from *targeted asset mapping*? We instill projects with hope, connectedness, and open-ended energy. For instance, it is not unusual to see people taking enthusiastic action on good ideas that have been on people's minds for a while. In conflict situations, some congregations have been amazed to find that asset mapping helps participants get past differences to focus on positive actions that everyone can support. In some cases, asset mapping has helped organized groups rediscover why they came together in the first place.

The openness of asset mapping means that ideas and interest will probably spill out into unexpected actions. We often end up with a different slate of tasks and efforts than we had before. A worship committee might get into something that looks like membership development, for example, while a membership group might take up something that looks like a social-justice ministry. Interest spillover like this is not a problem! It is a big success! It means that we are thinking about our connections to each other in community and faith.

Asset mapping helps participants get past differences to focus on positive actions that everyone can support.

Try to avoid pushing people and projects back into categories and cubbyholes. Do not eliminate options or prioritize them. You will fall back into the fixed-sum dynamic. Instead, give each other permission to act on interests and affinities as you see them. Have faith that this will accomplish your mission. If any two people want to work together, celebrate that and look for ways to connect their efforts to other assets and efforts. If any group finds a new course to get things done, experience that with wonder and joy. Together, you will experience a collective whole that is greater than the sum of the parts you each play in various committees and groups.

> **Q:** *Can we use asset mapping for strategic planning in our congregation?*
> **FSL:** Asset mapping works great with planning—before, during, or after. The open-sum approach ensures that planning works for faith in community.

If you have ever tried traditional planning with a congregation or faith-based organization, no doubt you have felt frustration. Asset mapping shows us why. We say we are all about putting control in God's hands (an open-sum approach), but then in planning we attempt to control things down to the last detail (a fixed-sum approach). We say we are committed to reaching out to everybody (open-sum), but we follow a planning approach that narrows things down, screens things out, and denies people's gifts and interests (fixed-sum). It is not surprising that plans often sit on a shelf.

The most strategic plan is the one that gets done. All the analysis and methodology in the world will not accomplish a thing if people do not recognize their contributions among the larger work of the congregation. In communities of faith, planning focuses on engaging the gifts and interests of members. In planning language, we are bottom-up, asset-based, and open-ended!

Congregations and faith organizations have used asset mapping in a variety of ways to support planning. Some have *started* with the Quick and Simple

Congregational Asset-Mapping Experience and then built on the spirit, vision, and practical results of that experience to guide subsequent planning.

I have seen other congregations use a version of the Quick and Simple Experience in the *middle* of planning. They had conversations about mission and values, then identified participant gifts and interests with asset mapping, and ended by planning potential actions to draw on those gifts to accomplish their mission. This approach is something like using the Optional Jumping-Off Point from chapter 4. We ask, "What is God's will for our community?" before starting with the other three steps of the Quick and Simple Experience.

The most strategic plan is the one
that gets done.

Finally, some groups have used The Quick and Simple Experience *after* a plan has been completed to discover ways to accomplish one or more of the planned objectives.

Regardless of when you use asset mapping, it helps you to steer clear of dead-ends in planning. You learn to assert the positive language of assets and gifts instead of needs and deficits, to build relationships around affinity instead of control, and to trust each other and God's goodness.

CONSULTANT'S JOURNAL
We are all in this together.

When I was recently asked to review the draft strategic plan of a religious organization, I found the plan a fascinating mix of open-sum and fixed-sum thinking.

The beginning of the document was rich and beneficent and entirely open-sum in language and content. As the planners proclaimed the organization's theological foundation and stated their vision, they repeatedly affirmed God's abundant gifts and grace. The plan said, "We are all in this together." It described each and all of us as tools for God's work on earth and located gatekeeping only in the hands of God. I loved the phrase, "Our vision is to catch up with what God is already doing in the world." You cannot get any more asset-based and open-sum than that!

The planners started mixing in fixed-sum thinking when they outlined their goals and objectives. The language and content sometimes included positive, thankful language, but often drew conclusions based on needs and weaknesses. These sections followed a general pattern. They started by saying that something was an important job (not a gift), then explained how they were failing at that job, and finally listed what they would like to accomplish to fix the problem.

For example, the plan described the congregations as formative communities, which could be an asset-based statement. Instead of identifying congregational strengths and ways to build on them, the document bemoaned perceived weaknesses, saying, "We must pay much greater attention to things like Bible study and organizational identity." Similarly, the plan proclaimed that evangelism is the "vocation of all the baptized," only to continue, "We do not do the ministry of evangelical outreach consistently well," and then named all the groups and types of people they had failed to reach.

I was fascinated by the places where assets and open-sum thinking seemed to hold sway over needs and fixed-sum approaches. Ecumenical and interfaith partnerships were described as "a vital medium for ministry." Diversity was described in strong asset language. In public ministry, "our collective voice" was identified as a strength to build on. In addition, a theology of grace, justice, and peace were described as "gifts to share with the world."

I suggested to the planners that the language of needs and weaknesses could easily be transformed to celebrate God's gifts and our opportunities for faithful service and witness. I think those suggestions were well received.

But I learned something from the experience that goes beyond the language of a particular plan. This plan reminded me of the constant struggle that faithful people face as we try to discern the will of God. Every day we face tensions between fixed-sum thinking and open-sum thinking. The many faithful people working together on a strategic plan are only human, but their successes and challenges are magnified and displayed to their whole community. Planning is a visible reminder to us that we strengthen each other's faith in community.

Faith Partnerships

Q: *We want to partner with other congregations but we do not know how to make it work. Can asset mapping help?*

FSL: Congregational asset mapping is an excellent framework for building bridges between congregations. Congregations have used the Quick and Simple Experience to develop or strengthen rural geographic cluster parishes, district or regional networks, community coalitions, global mission partnerships, ecumenical alliances, and other creative faith relationships. Regardless of the setting, open-sum thinking reminds us that faith partnerships are more than institutional arrangements; they are vehicles for building faith in community.

Business developers and lawyers follow a simple format when they negotiate partnerships. They ask, What does each side bring to the table, and what does each side take away? They try to match up these elements, see who gives

125

more or gets less, and even up the differences with money. They do not really have a way to put a price tag on assets like reputation, trust, or loyalty, so they note these things as intangibles and call it even.

Asset mapping gives two or more congregations a way to identify what they bring to the table, but instead of contrasting the differences, it helps them find the synergies, the gains that two groups can get from connecting their gifts. Asset mapping actually recognizes and strengthens intangibles like faith and community.

Sometimes one-sided relationships evolve between giver and recipient congregations. Typically, these relationships focus more on money than faith. Congregations can steer clear of this problem by using the Quick and Simple Experience to identify non-financial gifts that participants can use to get things done together. Singers might form a combined choir, for example, or travelers might exchange stories and cultural gifts. Members of the partner congregations might combine their voices to advocate for just government policies. The partners learn more about each other and about how to cooperate from these mutually beneficial arrangements.

Asset mapping also makes partnership more personal. When congregations partner as institutions, direct interaction is often limited to a few leaders. But when congregations map assets together, individuals are able to offer their own gifts to each other. Small groups form, friendships develop, and leaders see a broader vision of ministry than just policies and budgets. In one church, members of each congregation regularly traveled a long distance to visit and worship with each other. One couple that met through this partnership got married! Ultimately, partnerships between congregations are not institutional arrangements but efforts to find unity in God's family.

CONSULTANT'S JOURNAL
That's how I feel, too.
Leaders from several congregations gathered to share lessons and observations from their experiences in asset mapping. Some fascinating discussions focused on partnerships between congregations. Three urban congregations were part of a coalition. Two rural churches were yoking to share a pastor and other resources.

Marilyn, a lay leader from one of the yoking congregations said, "Believe it or not, the biggest issue for our people turned out to be the worship schedule. The congregations did not want to give up their time slots. We are alternating months now, switching early and late services at the two churches, but some people have said that it is too hard to remember."

Marilyn continued, "Since doing asset mapping together, I have noticed a change in attitude. We have gotten to know each other better and we are see-

ing some of the things we can do together that we could not do on our own. We have held services together. So last week, when I could not make it to the early service at Farmersburg, I went to the later service at MacGregor. I just thought, 'That's my church too.'"

Kris, a pastor from one of the urban congregations, thought about that a little and then said, "Instead of losing a time slot, you really gained a time slot. Seeing it from a personal perspective, Marilyn, your congregations are not just partners. You are one together."

"Kris, that's how I feel sharing these lessons with you, too." said Marilyn.

COMPASSION AND JUSTICE IN PUBLIC LIFE

Q: *We know we have been blessed with abundant gifts, but shouldn't we be giving to the needy?*
FSL: Of course we should be giving to others, but not because they are needy. We share what we have because we embrace God and love our neighbors. When we express concern for the needs of others, we are focusing on a half-empty cup—yet we are drawing a valuable connection to our brothers and sisters. Asset mapping builds on that connection and shows us something even bigger.

I believe that we all feel the tug of true compassion for those less fortunate than ourselves. Each of us makes a sincere, faithful effort to serve and give. Compassion is not just a sentiment of the privileged or wealthy. The poorest, most downtrodden, and unfortunate person imaginable will feel compassion for others and act on that compassion if given a chance. Often, the people who have little share the most.

Compassion leads us to two important realizations. First, compassion leads us to ponder our gifts. When we feel pity for others, we realize all that we have been given. When we raise funds for a sick child, for example, we are reminded of our own health or our own children. We recognize the value of gifts that we had taken for granted, and we thank God for our blessings.

Second, compassion turns us outward. We think less about our own self-interests and more about the interests of others. We realize a connection with others that widens our circle of interest. When we donate money and goods to the victims of a disaster halfway around the world, for example, we draw a connection that we never recognized before. Our compassion shows us that we are tied to our neighbors in an important way.

Asset mapping models both of these realizations—appreciating gifts and turning outward. And, asset mapping takes us a step further. Asset mapping leads us to the realization that God gifts us all and we are one in God's love.

Thinking about others' needs and focusing on charity has limitations. Even as compassion widens our circle of interest, charity distances us in a significant way from those we help. When we think that *they* are needy but *we* are gifted, we are casting *them* as different from *us*, and maybe even as less than us. We might be blessed with God's abundance, but when it comes to *them*, we do not think of God's abundance. Thinking about needs isolates us from the very people we seek to connect with. In its more extreme forms, this focus on needs dehumanizes our brothers and sisters in our own minds.

"Giving should affirm and not dehumanize," writes John M. Perkins, cofounder of the Christian Community Development Association, in his book *Beyond Charity: The Call to Christian Community Development* (Grand Rapids, Mich.: Baker Books, 1993; 28). "We give because God gave to us. We should be humbled by our opportunities to give" (ibid., 28).

Recall the needs transformation exercise we used with both the Personal Asset Starter and Recognizing Our Assets (in chapters 1 and 5). In that exercise, we look inside a need to find the asset that we care about. It is the asset, not the need, which shows us God's abundance and love and moves us to compassion. We give because God gave to us, not because God did not give to someone else! We share our gifts with each other because they all came from God in the first place, and we are all one in God. Our opportunities to give truly are humbling.

When needs become assets, they become part of us, and we all become servants of God.

We share what we have with the sick child because we care about her as a person, as part of our community, and as a child of God. She has gifts to share and contributions to make in our community. She is an asset herself. We stand with the people who are suffering because they are part of us.

We give to far-away disaster victims because we recognize that they, too, are children of God. They have gifts to share with the larger, global community. They are part of us, too, and all of us are part of something bigger.

When we stop thinking about other people as needy and instead think of all of us as gifted by God, we break down our isolation and embrace each other as brothers and sisters. When needs become assets, *they* become part of *us*, and we all become *servants of God*.

Asset mapping strengthens our compassion by helping us to make the step beyond charity to fellowship and witness. We move beyond filling the needs of other people. Instead, we recognize the affinities we share with neighbors near and far. Compassion is loving our neighbors.

Finally, asset mapping shows us that compassion is a model for action. Asset mapping helps us to discover ways to share our gifts in mutuality and fellowship. For example, besides giving money, we can work together with each other to make something of value, like a Habitat for Humanity home. We can redirect our personal and congregational budgets to buy products and services that build fairly on the talents and skills of our brothers and sisters. For example, we can buy fairly traded coffee. We can invest part of our endowment in local enterprises. We can join with other congregations to call for forgiveness of debt with developing nations. These options for compassion come from looking at assets instead of needs.

CONSULTANT'S JOURNAL
I learn what **self-help** *means.*

At Bethel New Life, the faith-based, inner-city community development corporation that I worked for straight out of business school, charity didn't enter into anything we did. Our visionary director, Mary Nelson, was not interested in filling needs, only building on community assets, and the same went for the resident board and constituency. For my part, I was given amazing opportunities to help develop and manage cutting-edge, grassroots, self-help, economic enterprises like a buy-back recycling venture and an energy-saving home-improvement loan center. With Kate Lane, our housing director, I made trips to partner congregations in the suburbs to market socially responsible investments in our affordable housing cooperatives.

I can imagine what it looked like to the people who came out to see us at our little pitch sessions in those comfortable church settings. Kate probably represented local flavor as an African American community resident who knew the people and the streets and testified to the good work of the organization. I no doubt was seen as the finance expert, the white guy with the degrees and credentials who could talk about taxes and rates of return to assure everyone that their investments were safe.

But that's not how it seemed to me. I was just the new guy, trying to figure out how to make my contribution and learning the ropes from Kate, the veteran developer who had made miracles work again and again.

After our presentations, some of the gathered faithful would always come up to me to ask personal questions. They would ask, "How do you like working there?" I told them it was hard work, but I really enjoyed it. The people were great, I was learning a lot, and I was grateful for the opportunity. They would press further, "Yes, but what's it like, really?" I laughed and said that it does get crazy sometimes, but it was all worth it for the amazing changes we saw. They asked, "How long do you plan to stay?" I told them that I didn't have any plans to leave, if that's what they meant.

> *Once, in the car on the way back to the neighborhood, I told Kate about these conversations and asked her if she knew what they were all about. "Of course, I do," she said. "But don't worry about it. They think you're doing us a big favor by coming to work at Bethel, a white guy with your fancy degrees."*
>
> *"Like I'd trade this for anything else," I laughed. Then I asked Kate why they questioned how long I was planning to stay.*
>
> *"They're church people. They think you must be on some sort of mission thing," she explained.*
>
> *I thought about that while we drove in silence, looking at the highway stretching ahead and the skyscrapers in the distance. The affluent suburban churchgoers thought I was making a sacrifice, taking some time out of my life to work in the ghetto. But I knew I had been given an amazing opportunity to play a part in something truly great with people like Kate. I didn't feel enno-bled by sacrifice. I felt enormously lucky. By going with Kate to the churches to market investments, I had the opportunity to model partnerships for people who might come to understand that everybody brings something to the table.*
>
> *Then I said to Kate, "A mission thing? Well, I think they've got that part right."*

Compassion and justice seem to come out of asset mapping without anybody telling anyone what to do. I have never seen a congregation focus the Quick and Simple Experience by saying, "Connect the dots to strengthen our compassion." Even so, asset mapping almost always leads us to strengthen our compassion. Participants often conceive and act on community ministries, not as self-interested outreach, but as mission. Even typically internal actions, like strengthening worship or stewardship, are approached with openness to the gifts of all. Leaders from seven congregations who participated in an early demonstration project on congregational asset mapping agreed that they were acting like churches without walls.

> **Q:** *How can we find the courage to act in the public sphere?*
> **FSL:** There is strength in the half-full cup. Asset mapping can help us to find our strength to speak and to witness to our faith in public. This might sound like a challenge, but actually public witness empowers us.

Sometimes we act as if faith should be be kept private. Sometimes we are afraid to speak up in public. Yet, we can hardly miss all the lessons in both the Old and New Testaments calling for us to proclaim a public witness to God's kingdom on earth.

CONSULTANT'S JOURNAL
It was the last thing he wanted to do.

A pastor spoke at our service club about his work in prison ministry. He said that when he was first invited to work with prisoners, facilitating Bible camps in prison was the last thing he wanted to do. He was afraid, and he did not want to go. He also did not want the people who invited him to think of him as either scared or unfaithful, so he went anyway. That was the beginning of 25 years in prison ministry. Now he organizes hundreds of lay and clergy to join him each year. He does not hesitate to let the lawmakers and the public know what he sees.

"I'm actually a shy person," he said. "You probably think of me differently, seeing me up here making a speech about my work in prisons. That is just the outside me. The inside me is nervous, uncomfortable, even scared." One thing that helped him, he said, was taking drama classes in school. "You have to learn to lie to be able to act. At the same time, drama really gets at the truth."

Interestingly, the half-full perspective supports our action in the public arena. I have been inspired to see asset-mapping participants vote with their feet to make a difference by challenging issues like race, gender, economic justice, and global equity. I have seen ordinary churchgoers take public action around everything from election campaigning to policy advocacy, from community organizing to worldwide mission development.

The truly wonderful and amazing thing to me is that asset mapping seems to lead us to public action, whether or not that's what we started out to do. Asset-mapping participants feel motivated and empowered to act in public without being told to do so. We act, not because of guilt or coercion, but as a witness to our faith. Asset mapping works like a hidden door to justice.

Each element of the Quick and Simple Experience gives us hope, power, and an ability to accomplish things. At the same time, each asset-mapping element teaches justice and equity. Running through all of it is a message about something bigger than human power and justice, something about God's love.

Recognizing Our Assets empowers us to act as individuals, and models the worth of every individual. Our fear of acting in public comes from a denial of our own gifts and assets, from seeing the cup as half-empty. We say things like, "What can I do?" and "No one will listen to me." We are afraid to act because we think we have no assets.

Recognizing Our Assets helps us conquer our personal fears by lifting up all that we have to use for action. Instead of saying, "What can I do?" and "No one will listen to me!" we say, "I do have a vote, a voice, skills, and spending power." We have many assets to use. We can make a difference.

When we rediscover the value of our own gifts, we are reminded both of the value of all of God's gifts and of the gifts and interests of others. In the

Quick and Simple Experience we see this immediately in the assets taped all over the wall. We recognize that each of us has something to contribute. We not only feel empowered, we see the individual worth of each person.

Connecting the Dots empowers us to act in concert with others and models loving our neighbors. Isolation discourages us from public action. Without connection to others, we feel insignificant. For instance, we question, "What difference does my vote make?" Connecting the Dots empowers us by illustrating how we can unite our assets to get things done. This understanding encourages us to reach out to each other, and we say things like, "There's strength in numbers."

Asset mapping works like
a hidden door to justice.

At the same time, Connecting the Dots shows us the common interests we have with each other as children of God. In the Quick and Simple Experience, we are able to brainstorm actions that take advantage of links between unlikely assets. Different assets contribute in different ways, and we have a common interest in finding useful connections. We say things like, "We have more in common than what divides us." We are not just empowered. We are loving our neighbors.

Voting with Our Feet empowers us to play a part in a larger movement, and models a love and justice that is bigger than all of us. Individuals react differently to the pressures of competition and control in public life. Some people may be attracted to the game, and others may be repelled. Still, there is no question that conflict takes its toll on all participants in a fixed-sum dynamic. None of us wants to be fighting over the crumbs.

We are empowered by Voting With Our Feet because we each contribute to a larger movement, a growing snowball of faith and action that none of us

---

Power and Justice in Asset Mapping
Recognizing Our Assets
- Empowers us to act as individuals
- Models the worth of every individual

Connecting the Dots
- Empowers us to act in concert with others
- Models loving our neighbors

Voting with Our Feet
- Empowers us as part of a larger movement
- Models a love and justice that is bigger than all of us

---

control but that all of us benefit from. In the Quick and Simple Experience, we look around in wonder at the collective capacity and energy of our whole group. We say, "The whole is greater than the sum of the parts."

At the same time, Voting with Our Feet shows us a glimpse of something beyond our control. We support each other in our calls, but we do not determine the results of our collective efforts. We witness the unexpected and are awed by the presence of a greater good. We sense that we are part of something bigger than any of us.

I've struggled with the language for this, how to name the "bigger thing." It is more than our love for each other or our human sense of justice on earth. What would you call it: God's justice, God's kingdom on earth, the church body, or the body of Christ? I have heard some people talk about agape, which I understand as God's love. Maybe the "bigger thing" is all of this and more. I just do not know enough to name it. Maybe you can.

To me, this bigger thing is a feeling. When people act together in community and faith, it feels to me like a spirit moving in the room. The bigger thing is not something we make, really, or something we have already. It is something in the space between our gifts, which we witness when our faith is active and open toward God. To me, this bigger thing feels like grace, grace between our gifts.

What I do know is this: Faith drives us to public witness. Asset mapping shows us that abundance, affinity, and release do more than just empower us; they lead us to recognize each other's individual worth, to love our neighbors, and to recognize that we are all part of something bigger. That's amazing. That makes my heart glad!

CONSULTANT'S JOURNAL
The congregation puts the hub in the wheel.

Pastor Scott and I talked on the phone a few weeks before I was scheduled to visit his small-town congregation for an asset-mapping workshop. We discussed the big issues for his congregation, and he said that his members were very capable and committed but seemed to look for direction. He also mentioned subjects like staff shortages, strained relationships with other churches, and local job losses. Then we got down to the issue of race.

"We're pretty much an all-white congregation in a mixed-race area," he said. "We've got a long-standing African-American community and a growing Spanish-speaking group here. But I'm not sure we're ready to get into all of that this session." I readily agreed with that. "We can hope this will open things up for future conversations," I said.

At the session, we all looked up after Voting with Our Feet to see lots of people standing next to several wonderful and creative actions. One woman stood alone at a cluster of assets entitled, Racial Diversity Training. One of the other groups saw this and took all their assets off the wall and moved them next to hers, saying, "If we're going to start a Job Clearinghouse, we're really going to benefit from Racial Diversity Training." The Disaster Relief Center group did the same thing, as did the groups working toward School Referendum Conversation and Worship Enhancement. Eventually, the whole agenda of those gathered was grouped like a wheel, with Racial Diversity Training at the hub.

In the months ahead, the congregation followed up on all of these actions, widened their circles of faith, and experienced benefits they never expected. I was awed and overjoyed. Although, I felt like kicking myself for thinking this community could not touch the issue of race and for underestimating the Holy Spirit.

EVANGELISM

Q: *Our people are good and faithful, but we have a hard time expressing our faith to others. How can asset mapping help us reach out to the unchurched and disassociated?*

FSL: I first heard these words of St. Francis of Assisi from a regular churchgoer who I would call an evangelist: "Preach the gospel always. If necessary, use words." Asset mapping gives ordinary lay people a way to preach the gospel in action first, then in words.

It is not always easy to share our faith with others. Our beliefs are deeply personal, and it can seem risky to expose them to others. We run the risk of being seen as proselytizers, perhaps. But when we experience the joy and wonder of God's grace, how can we help but want to share it with others?

---

*Asset mapping gives lay people a chance
to share their faith—successfully.*

Asset mapping gives individuals an opportunity to share their faith successfully. Congregations appreciate this. When we do asset mapping together, we see our own faith in action. We experience our own recognition of God's abundance, our own sharing of affinity with others, and our own release of control into the hands of God. When we do asset mapping, we see the results of what happens when we share our faith with others. We affirm each other and work together for the larger good. We practice "love thy neighbor," and it works.

CONSULTANT'S JOURNAL

We are Wednesday people. We are Sunday people.

The Prince of Peace congregation in a suburban Northwest community started a Wednesday afternoon after-school program by thinking about and building on their assets. They had adults who had an interest in children; neighborhood kids who had skills, interests, and time after school; and good space for both learning and recreation.

Connecting the dots, they recognized that Wednesday nights would be a good time to coordinate the regular gatherings of several church teams, peer support groups, and the youth group. Having these gatherings on one night made scheduling easier.

There was time available between the afternoon and the evening agendas, so why not serve food? People coming for the after-school program stayed a little later to eat, while people coming for the evening activities came a little earlier.

With everyone gathered for a meal, there was naturally an opportunity to ask a blessing. Then they added a song. Soon, they were having a brief worship service. The pastor led a Bible study after dinner. The participants, who now numbered over 100, were mostly from the community but not from the congregation, so they were getting to know the liturgy. This did not increase participation in the Sunday worship service. People who came on Wednesday did not come on Sunday.

One day an especially large number of people showed up for dinner, and there was not room for everyone to worship in the usual space. So the pastor suggested that the people move to the sanctuary. That was the turning point. Once the Wednesday participants were invited into the sanctuary, they began to see themselves as members of church. Baptisms, confirmations, and membership rose as the Wednesday people and the Sunday people become one people.

Asset mapping models faithful, loving action. The more we all gain, the more we want to connect that gain to others. We experience the growing, snowballing sensation of faith in community, and we want to do it some more. So congregations have found that participants want to share asset mapping with others. They want to try it at work or with a volunteer group.

One possible way to share faith is by facilitating the Quick and Simple Experience with groups we know. Asset mapping also can empower us to share our faith in less obvious ways. We discover that we can share our faith introducing the half-full cup in a group where we are discussing needs or deficiencies. We also can share our faith by seeking to understand other people's gifts and interests, so that we can connect assets with them for a larger good. When we join with others for a potluck supper, car pool, or a community clean-up project, we share our faith and practice our ministry in daily life.

To me, evangelism means inviting and welcoming wider circles of people into an open community of faith. Congregational asset mapping helps us model our open and relational faith in practice. It is "What you see is what you get." This kind of living witness attracts faith seekers to join our community.

CONSULTANT'S JOURNAL
The evangelist works.

It was a warm spring morning, the Sunday after Easter. The small, historic church I visited stands right in the middle of a crowded, lively, and very poor inner-city neighborhood. The doors to the sanctuary were wide open to the sun, and I walked in and took a seat next to Felicita. She is a quiet woman who speaks English as a second language, and she is a church leader who had attended my asset-mapping workshop the day before. She was to facilitate the Quick and Simple Experience with her church council members after the service.

As we waited for the service to begin, people drifted in and greeted each other like family. My mind was on the afternoon's scheduled session. Felicita's mind was on something else. She told me about her son, who had gotten caught up in the street life. Earlier that month he had been shot six times and left for dead. Felicita and Pastor Margaret sat by him in the hospital as he lay in a coma. After three days, Felicita told me, he opened up his eyes and looked at her and said, "Mom, I made it."

Three days, I thought, with a lump in my throat. I asked how he was doing now, and she told me that, incredibly, he was up and around. She could not see him or even be near him because the gangsters still threatened her son's life, and she might find herself in the path of more bullets. But she sometimes got word from him, through others on the street.

This is what has been on her heart, I thought, while I am training her to use the half-full cup. I told her how sorry I was for her pain and for her son's traumatic experience. But what Felicita wanted to tell me, insisting now, looking me in the eye, was how deeply she felt God's mercy and grace and how thankful she was for all of God's gifts.

Epilogue

An Asset Mapper Reads the Bible

I HAVE SEEN amazing things happen when people come together to share faith in community. Asset mapping has helped me to see these experiences reflected in the Bible. When I think about abundance, and affinity, and release, even the most well-known and loved passages from Scripture take on new light and meaning for me. I see that the Bible is present with us today.

I have learned to see signs of God's grace in my midst. I experience asset mapping less as an accomplishment, and more as a collective witness to grace. That makes me so glad I want to share it with others!

The Fullness of Grace

The Parable of the Talents

[Jesus said,] "For it is as if a man, going on a journey, summoned his [servants] and entrusted his property to them; to one he gave five talents, to another two, to another one, to each according to his ability. Then he went away. The one who had received the five talents went off at once and traded with them, and made five more talents. In the same way, the one who had the two talents made two more talents. But the one who had received the one talent went off and dug a hole in the ground and hid his master's money. After a long time the master of those [servants] came and settled accounts with them. The one who had received the five talents came forward, bringing five more talents, saying, 'Master, you handed over to me five talents; see, I have made five more talents.' His master said to him, 'Well done, good and trustworthy [servant]; you have been trustworthy in a few things, I will put you in charge of many things; enter into the joy of your master.' And the one with the two talents also came forward, saying, 'Master, you handed over to me

137

two talents; see, I have made two more talents.' His master said to him, 'Well done, good and trustworthy [servant]; you have been trustworthy in a few things, I will put you in charge of many things; enter into the joy of your master.' Then the one who had received the one talent also came forward, saying, 'Master, I knew that you were a harsh man, reaping where you did not sow, and gathering where you did not scatter seed; so I was afraid, and I went and hid your talent in the ground. Here you have what is yours.' But his master replied, 'You wicked and lazy [servant]! You knew, did you, that I reap where I did not sow, and gather where I did not scatter? Then you ought to have invested my money with the bankers, and on my return I would have received what was my own with interest. So take the talent from him, and give it to the one with the ten talents. For to all those who have, more will be given, and they will have an abundance; but from those who have nothing, even what they have will be taken away. As for this worthless [servant], throw him into the outer darkness, where there will be weeping and gnashing of teeth." (Matthew 25:14–30)

We often hear this story connected to stewardship or fundraising. I have always received and understood this general stewardship message: "Everything we have comes from God and will be returned to God. Don't bury your gifts in the backyard, but use them for God's will." I appreciated hearing that God's gifts need to be used for God's work. Reflecting on asset mapping, though, I think the message can be deepened.

What has bothered me about this parable is that the bad servant is the poorest servant. It seems backward to me. What about "the last shall be first" (Matthew 19:30) and "the meek shall inherit the earth" (Matthew 5:5)? Why

---

Why is the poorest servant the bad servant?
Maybe the point isn't how much we have,
but how much we think we have.

---

didn't the servant with 10 talents bury them and the servant with one talent do the right thing and enter into the master's joy? Wouldn't that have communicated the same lesson about appreciating and using God's gifts?

The story makes it clear that this apparent inequity is no mistake. Jesus said, "For to all those who have, more will be given, and they will have an abundance; but from those who have nothing, even what they have will be taken away" (Matthew 25:29). That seems terribly unfair. How is that God's justice?

In that verse, we have a clue. Jesus said that everything would be taken from the ones who have nothing. Now wait, how can you take away something from nothing? It's impossible. So maybe "those who have nothing" do have something after all.

Maybe the point is not how much we have, but how much we think we have. The servant with one talent had more than nothing, but he acted as though he had nothing. He did nothing with the talent. He did not even allow the money to earn interest.

The servant with one talent was looking at his cup as half-empty. He may have looked at the other two servants and thought, "Compared to them, I've got nothing." That is why the story includes the other two servants, to show how their more numerous talents could make the single talent seem insignificant to the third servant.

Then there is also the part about the one-talent servant's fear of a harsh master. The servant said that if he would have used the talent to buy, seek, and sow, the master might come and take away the harvest when it was grown. The way I read this, the one-talent servant said he was afraid his master would rob him! That's a pretty outrageous accusation to make against your master! But still more surprising, the master doesn't even contest the idea. "Maybe so," he seems to be saying, "But if you thought I was going to take away a harvest, you should have invested the talent with bankers." There are more and less risky things to do with my gifts, the master is saying, but that is no excuse for doing nothing. It is as if the master is saying, "You had my valuable gifts in your hand, and you didn't think they were valuable. You did not recognize and appreciate the assets you did have. You saw your cup as half-empty."

It's not the poor; it's poor mouthing that's the problem; looking over at the Joneses and saying we have nothing compared to them. Worrying about risk-

---

The servant saw his cup as half-empty.

---

ing what we have and failing to see the potential of our gifts—that is a problem. Jesus tells us not to take up a negative mind-set that leads us to overlook, underestimate, or take for granted God's gifts.

It depends on how we look at it. If we do not appreciate God's gifts, we live in the outer darkness and face the weeping and gnashing of teeth. From those that have nothing, even that will be taken away. That is a good description of some of the fixed-sum, vicious circles of denial and dissipation that we have all seen in our world.

But this story tells us that our talents, even a relatively small amount, are indeed valuable. We learn from what the master says to the two trustworthy servants—that if we appreciate and use God's gifts wisely, we will witness great gains we never expected. The fullness of God's grace is immeasurable and awesome.

The Wholeness of Grace

Psalm 23

> The LORD is my shepherd, I shall not want.
> He makes me lie down in green pastures;
> he leads me beside still waters;
> he restores my soul.
> He leads me in right paths for his name's sake.
> Even though I walk through the darkest valley,
> I fear no evil;
> for you are with me;
> your rod and your staff—they comfort me.
> You prepare a table before me
> in the presence of my enemies;
> you anoint my head with oil;
> my cup overflows.
> Surely goodness and mercy shall follow me all the days of my life,
> and I shall dwell in the house of the LORD
> my whole life long.

Psalm 23 is surely one of the best-known texts of the Judeo-Christian Scripture. This psalm of David is a gorgeous poem and a rich text. Like many people, I have often let the psalm's poetry wash over me with a message of God's power, grace, and mercy in my life. As I read it more closely, I comprehend lessons about sufficiency and abundance that reflect my experiences with asset mapping.

Which is it, sufficiency or abundance? Both messages seem to be right there in the text.

I shall not want. That is sufficiency in a nutshell. Whatever my situation, God will provide enough for me. If I am a sheep, the Lord is my shepherd. Follow the Lord, and I will get enough grass to eat and water to drink. I can appreciate those gifts and learn how to use them appropriately in God's family at this time, sufficient to my place.

My cup overflows. That is abundance in a nutshell. God's grace and gifts are wonderful, overwhelming, and infinite. God's goodness and mercy shall follow me all of my life. God's great power conquers evil and beats even death. God's gifts are so abundant that they go on forever and ever.

Now, which is the message of the psalm, that God's blessings are sufficient, or abundant? There is a big difference between having enough to get by, and receiving so much it never ends. But both messages seem to be right there in Psalm 23. What are we supposed to think?

I think the psalm suggests that abundance comes from sufficiency. First, we shall not want, then our cup overflows. What's more, I think I've seen this happen in the open sum dynamics of faith and community. Sufficiency turns into abundance, and it is amazing.

Think about what happens in asset mapping. We start with our own personal transformation of mind-set, from the half-empty cup to the half-full cup. Instead of thinking about what we do not have, we appreciate what we do have and use those gifts to get things done. Literally, we shall not want.

That shift in mind-set leads to the creation of new gifts. New possibilities open up when we connect our gifts with others. We create an ever-growing snowball of faith in community when we give each other permission to follow our hearts and place ourselves in God's hands. The more we give, the more we receive, and on and on, until our cup overflows.

Sufficiency is a mind-set or a way of thinking. Whatever gifts we have received from God, we can always worry that we do not have enough. But we

---

From the perspective of asset mapping, Psalm 23
is about more than sufficiency or abundance; it is about
our part in the larger whole of God's renewing grace.

---

can also choose to appreciate our gifts and their uses and to decide that they are enough. God's grace is sufficient.

When we act from sufficiency, we receive abundance. We see more making more making more. There is no end to what we can do when we use our gifts in faith with others. God's grace is truly abundant.

In asset mapping, we see that the half-full cup leads us to the renewing power of the open-sum dynamic. Learning from this experience, I understand Psalm 23 to be about more than sufficiency or abundance. It is about renewal. It says that the Lord restores my soul. The Lord feeds me and quenches my thirst with grasses and water that are restored in the natural cycle. I follow the Lord by making enough out of the Lord's gifts and the Lord follows me with mercy and goodness. The Lord leads me on the right path of renewal, and I dwell in the house of the Lord forever.

God's renewing grace is much bigger than me. God leads me by right paths for his name's sake, not my own. Even my enemies have gifts at the Lord's table and a place in the God's plan. God's opening, renewing, and infinite goodness and mercy even overcome the finality of human death, including mine. In God's grace, we are part of a larger whole. My home is a place in the house of the Lord—nothing more and, thank God, nothing less. And oh, it's good to be home.

The Presence of Grace

The Loaves and the Fishes

After this Jesus went to the other side of the Sea of Galilee, also called the Sea of Tiberias. A large crowd kept following him, because they saw the signs that he was doing for the sick. Jesus went up the mountain and sat down there with his disciples. Now the Passover, the festival of the Jews, was near. When he looked up and saw a large crowd coming toward him, Jesus said to Philip, "Where are we to buy bread for these people to eat?" He said that to test him, for he himself knew what he was going to do. Philip answered him, "Six months' wages would not buy enough bread for each of them to get a little." (John 6:1–7)

When it was evening, the disciples came to him and said, "This is a deserted place, and the hour is now late; send the crowds away so that they may go into the villages and buy food for themselves." Jesus said to them, "They need not go away; you give them something to eat." (Matthew 14:15–16)

They said to him, "Are we to go and buy two hundred denarii worth of bread, and give it to them to eat?" And he said to them, "How many loaves have you? Go and see." (Mark 6:37–38)

One of his disciples, Andrew, Simon Peter's brother, said to him, "There is a boy here who has five barley loaves and two fish. But what are they among so many people?" (John 6:8–9)

And [Jesus] said to his disciples, "Make them sit down in groups of about fifty each." (Luke 9:14)

Now there was a great deal of grass in the place; so they sat down, about five thousand in all. (John 6:10)

Taking the five loaves and the two fish, he looked up to heaven, and blessed and broke the loaves, and gave them to his disciples to set before the people; and he divided the two fish among them all. (Mark 6:41)

And all ate and were filled. (Luke 9:17)

When they were satisfied, [Jesus] told his disciples, "Gather up the fragments left over, so that nothing may be lost." So they gathered them up, and from the fragments of the five barley loaves, left by those who had eaten, they filled twelve baskets. (John 6:12–13)

Those who had eaten the loaves numbered five thousand men. (Mark 6:44)

When the people saw the sign that he had done, they began to say, "This is indeed the prophet who is to come into the world." (John 6:14)

A pastor friend of mine told me that the story of the loaves and the fishes is the only miracle included in all four books of the Gospel. In both Matthew and Mark a second, similar story is told again, with seven loaves and 4,000 people (Matthew 15:32–38 and Mark 8:1–9). And in both of those books the story comes up a third time, when the disciples say they have no bread, and Jesus reminds them of the first two incidences, saying, "Do you not understand?" (See Matthew 16:5–12 and Mark 8:11–21.) It seems pretty important!

I originally understood this story as a sign of Jesus' miraculous powers. Like walking on water and healing the sick, feeding the 5,000 is proof to us that Jesus is the Son of God. This still seems good and true to me. But I learned something more about the loaves and fishes by connecting it with asset mapping.

Sometime in my work on congregational asset mapping, I remembered an essay I had read several years before by Parker Palmer about the loaves and fishes story (*The Active Life: Wisdom for Work, Creativity, and Caring* [San Francisco: Harper San Francisco, 1991], 121–38). Palmer compared what Jesus did to what a community organizer would do, especially how Jesus broke the five thousand down into small groups of 50 for the disciples to work with. That got me thinking about what we do in the Quick and Simple Congregational Asset-Mapping Experience.

I read all four versions together, and the second and third tellings in Mark and Matthew, and I noticed details I hadn't seen before. The parallels between the loaves and the fishes and asset mapping drew me further into the text, and I began to imagine the scene:

The disciples start with a half-empty mind-set. They say they are in a deserted place, though we learn later there's grass enough for 5,000 people to sit comfortably. And the disciples start talking about money, another frequent sign of need thinking. The disciples say they don't have 200 denarii to pay to feed everyone. When the disciples suggest that Jesus send the people away to go buy something to eat, I wonder if everyone could afford to do that. It sounds more like the disciples are putting off any responsibility they might have for feeding the crowd.

Jesus won't let the disciples off the hook, saying in Matthew, "They need not go away; you give them something to eat." When the disciples ask how, Jesus asks the asset question: "How many loaves have you? Go and see." Go and see how much we have. That's what we do in Recognizing Our Assets. And how do we discover our gifts? By looking at the half-full cup.

In John's telling, it is a child who seems to make this personal transformation. A child has a supper of five loaves and two fish and offers it to Jesus and the disciples. Now, was this child the only one among 5,000 who brought food? Or was he just the only one who looked in his basket and saw what he had, instead of what he didn't have? What he had was some food, and he could appreciate the value of those gifts and take action, as a part of the community. This boy saw he could return God's gifts to God, and he did.

Jesus turns right around, blesses these gifts, and gives them to the 5,000. First he has the disciples organize people into small groups, as it says in Luke. Then, in Mark's words, "Taking the five loaves and the two fish, he looked up to heaven, and blessed and broke the loaves, and gave them to his disciples to set before the people." The boy shares his gifts, and Jesus passes them around in small groups, making sure everyone sees this act of giving and shares in this blessing.

What happens next in the small groups? It doesn't say—not in any of the four tellings of the story. Maybe Jesus waves a hand and makes food appear on everyone's plate. Maybe he does this as a sign of God's power and glory for the people who are gathered. But *if* the point is simply that Jesus can fix the problem, why does he start by asking the disciples to go and see what they had? And why bother with the small groups?

Mark and Matthew clearly rebuke the idea that the food came down like manna from heaven. After the first telling, when 5,000 are fed with five loaves, and a second telling, when 4,000 are fed with seven loaves, Mark and Matthew tell of a third event (Matthew 16:1–12 and Mark 8:11–21) that recapitulates the first two. The Pharisees and Sadducees ask for a sign, a miracle that will prove Jesus is the Son of God, and Jesus says no. Then disciples say they "have no bread" when they do indeed have a loaf. Jesus exclaims in Mark, "Why are you talking about having no bread? Do you still not perceive or understand? Are your hearts hardened? Do you have eyes, and fail to see?" (8:17–18). In Matthew, Jesus tells the disciples to "Beware of the yeast of the Pharisees and Sadducees" (16:11)! Matthew says, "Then they understood that he had not told them to beware of the yeast of bread, but of the teaching of the Pharisees and Sadducees," because they had asked Jesus for a sign from heaven (16:12).

It seems to me that Jesus is telling the disciples, and the crowds of 4,000 and 5,000 people, and all of us, not to see our cup as half empty and then depend on somebody to perform a miracle and fill our needs. In fact, he's pretty upset about that kind of thinking!

If it's clear that Jesus did not rain food down on the 5,000, how did everyone get fed? Where did the 12 leftover baskets come from? Maybe instead of waving his hand, Jesus started a ball rolling. He celebrated and held up the child's offer of his supper as an act of faith and love in community. He started Connecting the Dots, by passing out these gifts to everyone assembled. In small groups, maybe people were able to recognize and appreciate what they did have, and inspired by the child's act, contribute their own gifts to the group. Maybe they connected the dots. And when they did that, they discovered an abundance of food.

I said at the beginning that I originally saw the story of the loaves and fishes as a miracle story. Now it might sound like I'm saying that no miracle occurred and the 5,000 were fed with their own food. I guess there's room in the Bible for either interpretation. But I think there's a third way of looking at the story.

Jesus never ordered anyone to do anything, nor did the disciples. They didn't set priorities or screen people based on needs. Instead, I think each person gave the others permission to follow their hearts. They followed their hearts to contribute and gain in community.

Then the unexpected happened. From a crowd that had nothing, everyone was fed. And from the growing snowball of faith and action, still more was created and left over, more than enough to start all over again with the next meal!

I think it really was a miracle. Not a test or a demonstration that happened once 2,000 years ago, but something amazing that's here and present today. I feel this miracle every time I witness groups of people rediscovering assets, finding affinities with each other, and making things happen by giving each other permission to follow their hearts.

What I've learned from working with people like you is that there is a real miracle present among us in community. This miracle is active whenever we live and work together in faith. There's Spirit moving in and among us, revealing its power to us when we act on our faith and our love for each other. There's grace between our gifts.

What a joy and a wonder that is for us. We already know how to act in faith and community with each other. Asset mapping gives us a reminder, an encouragement, and a permission. Let's celebrate, and do it some more!

Coda

I imagine myself in the crowd of 5,000, looking for the child who had five loaves and two fish. I don't know who the boy was. He was just a regular person like all of us, a face in a crowd of 5,000. He never met Jesus, or was touched by Jesus. The Bible doesn't even tell us the child's name.

And yet, he took the action that mattered, in the miracle that that is celebrated so highly in the New Testament. His was the simple act of faith that turned that crowd into a community.

He could be any of us. He could be all of us.

I imagine myself wading through the crowd, searching for the child. Finally, I find him in one of the small groups, with his circle of friends and neighbors now widened to include strangers who also came to hear Jesus. I see him taking his place to eat with the others, and I ask him about his five loaves and two fish. I say, "This was your supper, your feast. How could you afford to give that to all these people?"

And I imagine this child answering, "This was my supper, my feast. How could I afford not to?"

Hallelujah!

Appendix

Resources for Further Exploration

I LEARNED ABOUT asset mapping from living and working in community and faith with people like you. Together we make up a movement. From time to time, I find out more about the extent and reach of our movement through like-minded colleagues. People approach me after a workshop and tell me about a book or a speaker who reminds them of asset mapping. Here are a few resources you might follow to dig deeper into aspects of what we have discussed in this book.

Asset-Based Community Development

This book, *The Power of Asset Mapping,* builds on the ideas and practices of Asset-Based Community Development. These are some other works for people interested in ABCD.

The single most widely read and discussed book on Asset-Based Community Development is still the original:

Kretzmann, John P. and John McKnight. *Building Communities from the Inside Out: A Path toward Finding and Mobilizing a Community's Assets.* Evanston, Ill.: Asset-Based Community Development Institute, 1993. Distributed by ACTA Publications, 4848 N. Clark Street, Chicago, IL 60640. Phone: (800) 397-2282; e-mail: actapublications@aol.com.

There are a series of follow-up publications to this book, available from the same distributor. I wrote two of them that you might find of interest. For rural communities, there is:

Snow, Luther K. *The Organization of Hope: A Workbook for Rural Asset-Based Community Development.* Evanston, Ill.: The ABCD Institute and The Blandin Foundation, 2001.

For those who are interested in how grassroots organizations tackle large-scale economic development projects there is:

Snow, Luther K. *Community Transformation: Turning Threats into Opportunities.* Evanston, Ill.: The ABCD Institute, Bethel New Life, Inc., and the Chicago Association of Neighborhood Development Organizations, 2001.

A third book in the ABCD series is an excellent resource on the connections between ABCD and faith communities. I contributed a chapter to this book on the story of the National Demonstration Project on Congregational Asset Mapping for the Evangelical Lutheran Church in America. This book also contains the best listing I have seen of scriptural texts on assets and community:

Rans, Susan and Hilary Altman. *Asset-Based Strategies for Faith Communities*. Illustrated by Dan Erlander. Evanston, Ill.: The ABCD Institute, 2002.

Theory and Theology

These are books for people who are interested in the ideas of open-sum thinking, learning by doing, and the theology of power and justice.

Open-sum thinking finds parallels in various fields, especially in the win-win modeling of game theory and negotiation analysis. The broadest and most comprehensive exploration of open-sum thinking that I have seen is actually a work of deep religious philosophy:

Carse, James P. *Finite and Infinite Games: A Vision of Life as Play and Possibility*. New York: Ballantine Books, 1986.

I've tried to show how asset mapping connects with learning by doing. I've also discussed how asset mapping leads to action for power and justice. So it's not surprising that the classic work about learning by doing is also a compelling examination of power and justice from the bottom up:

Freire, Paolo. *Pedagogy of the Oppressed*. New York: Herder and Herder, 1970.

I also appreciate a volume of essays by educators who are wrestling with the other side of the same coin:

Evans, Alice Frazer, Robert A. Evans, and William Bean Kennedy. *Pedagogies for the Non-Poor*. Maryknoll, N.Y.: Orbis Books, 1994.

On the implications of faith in God's love for power and justice, look at the works of Dietrich Bonhoffer and Paul Tillich, especially:

Tillich, Paul. *Love, Power, and Justice: Ontological Analyses and Ethical Applications*. London: Oxford University Press, 1954.

Congregational Practice

These are some books that explore how like-minded theologies and theories enlighten practical aspects of congregational development.

This book captures the spirit and many of the methods of asset mapping in real-world congregational settings:

Sitze, Bob. *Not Trying Too Hard: New Basics for Sustainable Congregations*. Bethesda, Md.: The Alban Institute, 2001.

147

For a careful consideration of the applications of learning by doing to congregations, consider:

Dennis G. Campbell. *Congregations as Learning Communities: Tools for Shaping Your Future*. Bethesda, Md.: The Alban Institute, 2000.

The successes of community-based organizing provide a strong practical guide for efforts to build power and achieve justice. One book that really opens up the connection with communities of faith is:

Jacobsen, Dennis A. *Doing Justice: Congregations and Community Organizing*. Minneapolis: Fortress Press, 2001.

This book incorporates several related theories with recommendations for opening up congregations, including thinking about organizational cycles:

Foss, Michael W. *A Servant's Manual: Christian Leadership for Tomorrow*. Minneapolis: Fortress Press, 2002.

Finally, the writer and consultant who pulls all this together in spirit and practice for me is Peter Block. He infuses open-sum thinking into expert perspective on organizational development and individual leadership:

Block, Peter. *Stewardship: Choosing Service over Self-Interest*. San Francisco: Berrett-Koehler Publishers, 1993.
———. *The Answer to How Is Yes*. San Francisco: Berrett-Koehler Publishers, 2002.

Networks

Besides reading good books, I also recommend getting involved in networks and associations of like-minded people. I recommend two national associations in particular that I think might be helpful to you in networking and sharing with other asset mappers:
Christian Community Development Association. Web site: http://www.ccda.org
National Community Building Network. Web site: http://www.ncbn.org

As you do your own asset building for faith and community, I hope you will discover other resources that help, and maybe create a few of your own. I would love to hear about your discoveries and creations. Contact me through the Alban Institute (Web site: http://www.alban.org) or send me an e-mail at luthersnow@hotmail.com. Thanks.